BRITISH COASTAL SHIPS
TUGS AND TRAWLERS

BRITISH COASTAL SHIPS TUGS & TRAWLERS

Gilbert I. Mayes

LONDON

IAN ALLAN LTD

Frontispiece: BROODBANK, Port of London Authority *P.L.A*

First published 1975

ISBN 0 7110 0592 3

Published by Ian Allan Ltd, Shepperton, Surrey
and printed in the United Kingdom by
Redwood Burn Limited
Trowbridge and Esher

CONTENTS

ABBREVIATIONS

General

DE	Diesel with electric drive
M	Diesel
SCH	Schottel overstern directional unit
SR	Steam reciprocating, compound or triple expansion
SRT	Steam reciprocating with L.P. turbine
ST	Steam turbine
TE	Steam turbine with electric drive
VS	Voith-Schneider cycloidal propeller
(A)	Machinery aft
(2) (3)	Twin screw, Triple screw
(PW)	Paddle wheel
(F & A)	Propellers forward and aft
dw	Deadweight tonnage

In Tug Section

FF	Fitted with Fire Fighting monitors
K	Kort nozzle fitted around propeller or Kort rudder
M rbt	
fm SR	Steam reciprocating machinery replaced with diesel
Pshr	Pusher tug
SAL	Fitted with salvage equipment and additional accommodation
(B)	Brake horse power
(I)	Indicated horse power

Trawler Port Registry Letters and Numbers

All fishing vessels bear Port Registry letters and numbers on each bow and on larger vessels additionally on the quarter. Identification is simplified by the inclusion of these in the text, where the following will be found.

A	Aberdeen	**GW**	Glasgow	**LO**	London
BCK	Buckie	**GY**	Grimsby	**LT**	Lowestoft
BM	Brixham	**H**	Hull	**M**	Milford Haven
FD	Fleetwood	**HL**	Hartlepool	**PZ**	Penzance
FR	Fraserburgh	**KY**	Kircaldy	**SN**	South Shields
GN	Granton	**LH**	Leith	**YH**	Gt. Yarmouth

Notes on Description of Funnel and Hull Colours

In describing funnel and hull colours, terms such as 'lemon' and 'buff' have been avoided, the generic term yellow being used throughout. Similarly, the term 'red' has been used to cover a wide variety of shades. With respect to funnel markings, the term 'band' has been used in preference to 'ring', this term only being used to denote a circular marking on the side of the funnel.

The colours listed are those normally used by the owning company and it must be borne in mind that vessels may from time to time be chartered to other operators and appear in the chartering company's livery. Where such an arrangement has some degree of permanence, the fact has been noted. Foreign flag coasters may also be encountered in the colours of a British operator while on charter and this is noted where it is regular practice.

It has not proved possible to obtain the funnel markings and hull colours of all the companies listed in the book and space has been left in these instances to enable the individual to insert these at a later date.

INTRODUCTION

With this latest edition of British Coastal Ships, Tugs and Trawlers, opportunity has been taken to revise and correct the material completely, whilst still retaining the successful format of previous editions.

The book has been divided into the following sections with further sub-division for Irish flag vessels. A single index has been provided for the whole book.

Coastal and Short Sea Passenger and Cargo Ships. Vessels listed in this section will generally be found trading coastwise or engaged in trade with Scandinavian and Continental ports, although some companies who trade through to the Mediterranean have also been included. For the sake of completeness several fleets list vessels that may well be found further afield, usually when engaged on charter work. Other companies in this section operate in a much more restricted area, notably sand and gravel dredgers, some eustuaral tankers and barges.

Pilot, Lighthouse and Buoy Tenders. Included in this section are vessels of Trinity House and other lighthouse and harbour authorities which operate craft of this type over 200 gross tons.

Oil Rig Servicing, Safety and Supply vessels and Research vessels. This is a rapidly expanding field and unavoidably some fleet lists may change considerably as older units are sold and replaced with more sophisticated vessels. Vessels from this section may be engaged on contract work in other parts of the world.

Harbour Works and Dredging Craft. Vessels included in this section have been restricted to self-propelled dredgers (with a note on the type of equipment installed) and hopper barges which in the main work with dumb dredging plant.

Tugs. An attempt has been made to include all tugs of over 30 gross tons with the exception of some units which are laid-up or privately owned and do not operate commercially.

Trawlers. This final section deals with all fishing vessels of over 100 gross tons with the exception of a few units that no longer fish commercially. In some trawler fleet lists, difficulty has been experienced in keeping pace with the changes in ownership or management of vessels by subsidiary companies although every effort has been made to ensure accuracy.

Inevitably in a book of this kind, changes take place between the preparation of the manuscript and the date of publication and some errors and omissions will occur. Where possible, known changes in companies and fleet lists have been noted in the Addenda.

Acknowledgements are due to the Shipping Companies, Lloyd's Register, Olsen's Almanac, the World Ship Society, the Maritime Institute of Ireland and to many others who have given help with information and photographs.

Gilbert I. Mayes

April, 1974

COASTAL AND SHORT SEA PASSENGER AND CARGO SHIPS

ABERDEEN COAL & SHIPPING CO LTD
Aberdeen

FUNNEL: Black with white band between two red bands.
HULL: Black with red boot-topping and white line.

Name	Built	Tons	Length	Breadth	Speed	Engines
Ferryhill II	1971	199	137	25	9	M(A)

ALBRIGHT & WILSON LTD
(Marchon Products Ltd)

Whitehaven

FUNNEL: Blue with red letters "MP" on red bordered white disc.
HULL: Grey with red boot-topping.

Name	Built	Tons	Length	Breadth	Speed	Engines
Marchon Enterprise	1962	1,599	261	39	12	M(A)
Marchon Venturer	1962	1,599	261	39	12	M(A)

ALDERNEY SHIPPING CO LTD
Alderney, C.I.

FUNNEL: Blue with white bird.
HULL: Blue with red boot-topping.

Name	Built	Tons	Length	Breadth	Speed	Engines
Sea Trent ex Seacon-71	1968	200	146	24	10¼	M(A)
Link Services Ltd:						
Alderney Courier ex Reiger 70, Wilca-65, Rejo- 55, Wim-54, Tasman	1940	203	116	22	7½	M(A)

ALGINATE INDUSTRIES (SCOTLAND) LTD

Inverness

FUNNEL:
HULL:

Name	Built	Tons	Length	Breadth	Speed	Engines
Alga ex Klydon-69	1963	116	82	20	9½	M(A)

ALLANTONE SUPPLIES LTD
(Gaselee & Son (Felixstowe) Ltd)

Felixstowe

FUNNEL: Blue with red letter "A" and black top.
HULL: Black.

Name	Built	Tons	Length	Breadth	Speed	Engines
Coastal Bunkering Tankers:						
Contractor ex Regent Wren-71	1950	161	121	19	7	M(A)
Contributor ex Beagle Venturer-73, Kendale H.	1960	256	140	22	7½	M(A)
Conveyor ex Broachdale H.-71	1953	162	139	18	7½	M(A)

ALLIED MILLS LTD

Gloucester

FUNNEL: Black with yellow band between narrow brown bands.
HULL: Black.

Name	Built	Tons	Length	Breadth	Speed	Engines
Severn Side	1952	244	134	21	7½	M(A)

J. A. ANDERSON

Eastbourne

FUNNEL:
HULL:

Name	Built	Tons	Length	Breadth	Speed	Engines
Gena ex Spray-70 Johanna-64, Friedi–52, Gruno–52	1930	239	130	22	8½	M(A)

ANSCAR SHIPPING LTD

Immingham

FUNNEL & HULL: Operating in colours of Roto Line, Wallhamn, Sweden.
(Funnel: White with Roto Line symbol in green).

Name	Built	Tons	Length	Breadth	Speed	Engines
Valerie	1972	3,390	429	53	14¾	M(A)

ANTLER LTD

Hamilton, Bermuda

FUNNEL: Yellow with white letter "A" on red and blue panel.
HULL: Black with red boot-topping.

Name	Built	Tons	Length	Breadth	Speed	Engines
Willmary	1966	199	137	25	8½	M(A)

ARC MARINE LTD

(Amey Roadstone Corp Ltd)

(*A member of the Goldfields Group*)

Southampton

FUNNEL: Blue with broad white band or blue.
HULL: Black or dark blue with red boot-topping.

Name	Built	Tons	Length	Breadth	Speed	Engines
Sand Dredgers and Carriers:						
Allard ex Mallard-64, West Coaster-50	1938	364	143	25	9	M(A)
Arco Avon ex Pen Avon-73	1966	787	188	34	11	M(A)
Arco Dart ex Pen Dart-73, Sand Dart-64	1957	499	165	30	10	M(A)
Arco Scheldt ex Amey III-73	1972	1,583	251	46	12½	M(A)
Arco Severn	1973	1,599	267	46	12	M(A)
Arco Tamar ex Wm. Woolaway-73	1964	355	146	29	10	M(A)
Arco Taw ex Pen Taw-73	1968	349	146	29	10	M(A)
Arco Test ex Amey II-73	1971	594	200	32	11	M(A)
Arco Thames	1974	1,645	—	—	13	M(A)
Arco Trent ex Amey I-73	1971	594	200	32	11	M(A)
Arco Yar ex Pen Yar-74, Laga II-69	1955	671	172	35	9	M(A)
Eko	1943	181	113	22	7	M(A)
Friargate	1934	246	116	23	8	M(A)
New (2)	1974					M(A)

See also Tugs, and Comben Longstaff & Co. Ltd.

Name	Built	Tons	Length	Breadth	Speed	Engines
Ellen B. ex Wocester- brook-72	1958	1,095	218	34	11	M(A)
Frances B. ex Blisworth-71	1957	1,031	213	34	10½	M(A)
Seabright Shipping Ltd: (Funnel: Divided vertically, blue white, blue, with blue and white "Seahorse" motif on white)						
Pauline H. ex Pearl-72	1953	1,093	212	34	10½	M(A)

C. A. BRINDLE
(Dale Sand & Gravel Co Ltd)

Cowes, I.O.W.

FUNNEL: Dark blue with red top separated by narrow white band.
HULL: Blue with red boot-topping.

Name	Built	Tons	Length	Breadth	Speed	Engines
Sand Dredger and Carrier:						
Sir Cedric ex Pen Arun-73, Lantyan, Roselyne	1943	311	141	21	8	M(A)

BRISTOL STEAM NAVIGATION CO LTD
(Lovell's Shipping & Transport Group)

Bristol

FUNNEL: Yellow with houseflag (White with red St. Andrew's Cross and blue letters "B.S.N.C." in each quarter).
HULL: Black with white line and red boot-topping.

Name	Built	Tons	Length	Breadth	Speed	Engines
Apollo	1954	1,254	278	39	10½	M(A)
Echo	1957	1,241	278	40	12½	M(A)

BRITISH DREDGING (SHIPPING) LTD

London, Bristol & Cardiff

FUNNEL: White with black top and houseflag.
HULL: Black with red boot-topping.

Name	Built	Tons	Length	Breadth	Speed	Engines
Sand Dredgers and Carriers:						
Badminton	1956	610	154	33	9½	M(A)
Bowbelle	1964	1,486	262	45	11½	M(A)
Bowcrest	1955	587	179 ·	30	9½	M(A)
Bowcross	1967	959	196	39	10	M(A)
ex Chichester Cross-71						
Bowfleet	1965	1,548	265	45	11½	M(A)
Bowline	1953	596	179	29	9½	M(A)
Bowqueen	1963	1,317	258	40	12½	M(A)
Bowsprite 🏴	1967	1,503	264	46	12½	M(A)
Bowstar	1950	561	169	28	9½	M(A)
British Dredging (Sand & Gravel) Co Ltd:						
Bowherald ✓	1973	2,965	325	60	12	M(A)
Bowknight	1973	2,965	325	60	12	M(A)
Bowstream ✓	1971	1,330	236	43	12½	M(A)
ex Hudson Stream-72						
Bowtrader ✓	1969	1,592	283	48	12	M(A)
Bristol Sand & Gravel Co Ltd:						
Peterston	1961	748	176	33	11	M(A)

BRITISH RAILWAYS BOARD
(Shipping & International Services Div)
and other companies operating as
SEALINK
FUNNEL: Red with black top and British Rail "Twin-Arrow" device, except
as follows: S.N.C.F.: Yellow with black top (with addition of ex L.B.S.C. houseflag on Newhaven-Dieppe vessels); Belgian Marine: Yellow with black top
separated by red over white over blue bands; A.L.A.: "ALA" monogram
instead of "Twin-Arrow".
HULL: Dark blue with or without white line separating red boot-topping
and large name "SEALINK" in white amidships in passenger vessels.

Name	Built	Tons	Length	Breadth	Speed	Engines
Passenger and Car Ferries:						
Avalon	1963	6,706	404	60	21	ST(2)
Caesarea	1960	3,992	322	54	18	ST(2)
Cambria	1949	5,284	397	56	18	M(2)
Dover	1965	3,602	369	57	19½	ST(2)
Duke of Argyll	1956	4,450	376	57	19	ST(2)
Duke of Lancaster	1956	4,450	376	57	19	ST(2)
Duke of Rothesay	1956	4,138	376	57	19	ST(2)
Falaise	1947	2,416	311	50	20½	ST(2)
Hengist	1972	5,590	385	65	19½	M(2)
Hibernia	1949	5,284	397	56	18	M(2)
Holyhead Ferry I	1965	3,879	369	57	19½	M(2)
Horsa	1972	5,590	385	65	19½	M(2)
Lord Warden	1952	3,333	362	61	19½	ST(2)
Maid of Kent	1959	3,920	373	61	19½	ST(2)
Maid of Orleans	1949	3,796	342	52	19½	ST(2)
Normannie	1952	2,219	309	50	19½	ST(2)
Sarnia	1961	3,989	322	54	18	ST(2)
Senlac	1973	5,590	385	65	19½	M(2)
St. Edmund	1973	9,000	430	74	21	M(2)
St. George	1968	7,356	420	67	21	M(2)
British Transport Ship Management (Scotland) Ltd:						
Ailsa Princess	1971	3,715	369	57	19½	M(2)
Antrim Princess	1967	3,630	369	57	19½	M(2)
Dalriada* ex Stena Trailer-71	1971	1,599	349	54	17	M(2)(A)
Ulidia ex Stena Carrier -74	1970	1,599	347	53	17	M(2)(A)
Belgian State Marine (Belgian flag):						
Artevelde Koningin	1958	2,812	383	49	22	M(2)

* *On Charter*

Name	Built	Tons	Length	Breadth	Speed	Engines
Elizabeth	1957	3,389	374	47	24	M(2)
Koningin Fabiola	1962	3,057	382	50	22	M(2)
Prince Laurent	1974	5,000	385	63	22	M(2)
Prins Philippe	1973	5,000	385	63	22	M(2)
Prinses Josephine Charlotte	1949	2,572	372	44	22	M(2)
Princesse Astrid	1968	3,188	384	50	22	M(2)
Prinses Paola	1966	4,356	389	49	22	M(2)
Reine Astrid	1958	3,389	374	47	24	M(2)
Roi Baudouin	1965	3,241	384	50	22	M(2)
Roi Leopold III	1956	3,389	375	47	24	M(2)

Fishguard & Rossiare Railways & Harbour Co:

Name	Built	Tons	Length	Breadth	Speed	Engines
Caledonian Princess	1961	3,630	353	57	19	ST(2)

Soc. Nat. des Chemins de Fer Francais (French flag):

Name	Built	Tons	Length	Breadth	Speed	Engines
Chantilly	1965	3,400	361	59	$19\frac{1}{2}$	M(2)
Chartres	1974	5,000	371	61	$20\frac{1}{2}$	M(2)
Compiegne	1958	3,467	377	60	$19\frac{1}{2}$	M(2)
Valencay	1965	3,433	344	56	19	M(2)
Villandry	1965	3,430	344	56	19	M(2)

Vehicle Ferry:

Name	Built	Tons	Length	Breadth	Speed	Engines
Capitaine Le Goff	1972	499	296	49	16	M(2)(A)

Stoomvaart Maats. "Zeeland" (Netherlands flag):

Name	Built	Tons	Length	Breadth	Speed	Engines
Koningin Juliana	1968	6,682	430	67	21	M(2)
Koningin Wilhelmina	1960	6,228	394	57	21	M(2)

Train Ferries:

Name	Built	Tons	Length	Breadth	Speed	Engines
Anderida	1972	1,579	355	54	17	M(2)(A)
Cambridge Ferry	1963	3,294	403	61	$13\frac{1}{2}$	M(2)
Essex Ferry	1957	3,089	400	61	$13\frac{1}{2}$	M(2)
Norfolk Ferry	1951	3,157	399	61	$13\frac{1}{2}$	M(2)
Suffolk Ferry	1947	3,134	405	62	$13\frac{1}{2}$	M(2)
Vortigern	1969	4,371	376	63	$19\frac{1}{2}$	M(2)

S.A. de Nav. Angleterre-Lorraine-Alsace (French flag):

Name	Built	Tons	Length	Breadth	Speed	Engines
St. Eloi	1974	4,500	376	61	$19\frac{1}{2}$	M
Twickenham Ferry	1934	2,839	360	63	15	ST(2)

Soc. Nat. des Chemins de Fer Francais (French flag):

Name	Built	Tons	Length	Breadth	Speed	Engines
St. Germain	1951	3,094	380	61	$18\frac{1}{2}$	M(2)

Sealink (Continued)

Name	Built	Tons	Length	Breadth	Speed	Engines
Cargo Ships:						
Brian Boroime	1970	4,098	352	57	$14\frac{1}{2}$	M(2)(A)
Colchester†	1959	1,946	296	38	$13\frac{1}{2}$	M(A)
Container Enterprise	1958	1,000	263	42	$12\frac{1}{2}$	M(A)
Container Venturer	1958	1,000	263	42	$12\frac{1}{2}$	M(A)
Isle of Ely	1958	1,492	241	38	$13\frac{1}{2}$	M(A)
Rhodri Mawr	1970	4,095	352	57	$14\frac{1}{2}$	M(2)(A)
Sea Freightliner I	1968	4,034	388	55	$13\frac{1}{2}$	M(2)(A)
Sea Freightliner II	1968	4,034	388	55	$13\frac{1}{2}$	M(2)(A)
Slieve Donard	1959	1,569	310	47	$13\frac{1}{2}$	M(2)
Soc. Nat. des Chemins de Fer Francais (French flag):						
Transcontainer I	1968	2,760	341	61	15	M(2)(A)
Isle of Wight Ferries:						
Brading	1948	986	200	48	12	M(2)
Caedmon	1973	764	198	51	9	M(F & A)
Camber Queen	1961	293	166	43	9	M(F & A)
Cenred	1973	761	198	51	9	M(F & A)
Cenwulf	1973	761	198	51	9	M(F & A)
Cuthred	1969	704	196	52	9	M(F & A)
Fishbourne	1961	293	166	43	9	M(F & A)
Freshwater	1959	363	164	43	9	M(F & A)
Shanklin	1951	986	200	48	12	M(2)
Southsea	1948	986	200	48	12	M(2)
Lake Windermere Service:						
Swan	1938	251	142	26	11	M(2)
Swift	1900	203	158	22	11	M
Teal	1936	251	142	26	11	M(2)
Tern	1891	120	146	19	11	M
Tilbury–Gravesend Ferries:						
Cathrine	1961	214	110	28	$9\frac{1}{4}$	M(2)
Edith	1961	214	110	28	$9\frac{1}{4}$	M(2)

* *On charter*

† *Chartered out under outside management*

See also Associated Humber Lines Ltd

BRITISH ROAD SERVICES LTD

Newport, I.O.W.

FUNNEL: Yellow with black top separated by narrow green band.
HULL: Black with green top line and "BRITISH ROAD SERVICES" in white.

Name	Built	Tons	Length	Breadth	Speed	Engines
Covert	1950	133	81	20	8	M(2)(A)
Northwood	1962	171	100	23	$8\frac{1}{2}$	M(2)(A)

Also motor vessels, Cowes and Needles

T. R. BROWN & SONS LTD

Bristol

FUNNEL: Black with broad red band between narrow white bands.
HULL: Black with green or red boot-topping, or black.

Name	Built	Tons	Length	Breadth	Speed	Engines
Sand Carriers and Dredgers:						
Severn Bridge	1936	165	103	21	7	M(A)
Sheperdine	1949	170	100	21	7	M(A)
Alexander McNiel & Co, Greenock:						
Colonsay ex VIC 63-56	1945	146	81	20	7	M(A)
Norwest Sand & Ballast Co Ltd, Liverpool:						
Norstar	1961	614	156	36	9	M(A)
Norwest	1955	586	152	35	$9\frac{1}{2}$	M(A)
The Holms Sand & Gravel Co, Bristol:						
Harry Brown	1962	634	172	33	$10\frac{1}{2}$	M(A)
Norleader ✓	1967	1,600	240	44	12	M(A)

See also Tugs

Top: HENGIST, British Railways Board *J. Clarkson*

LA QUINTA, Buries Markes Ltd *J. K. Byass*

A. J. BUSH LTD
(Maldon Shipping Co Ltd)

Maldon

FUNNEL: Green with yellow letter 'B' between narrow yellow bands.
HULL: Green with white topline and black boot-topping.

Name	Built	Tons	Length	Breadth	Speed	Engines
Sand Dredgers and Carriers:						
Doddles ex Admiralty X-Lighter	1915	121	98	20	7	M(A)·
Purbeck	1936	199	103	24	8½	M(A)

BULK CARGO HANDLING SERVICES LTD
(A Subsidiary of the Alexandra Towing Co Ltd)

Liverpool

FUNNEL: Black with red letters "BCHS" on red bordered white panel on broad blue band between narrow white bands.
HULL: Black with red boot-topping or * grey with red boot-topping.

Name	Built	Tons	Length	Breadth	Speed	Engines
Agnes	1913	187	96	22	8	M(A)
Anderton	1946	285	98	23	8	M(A)
Barnton	1945	285	98	23	8	M(A)
D. W. Williams	1919	177	96	23	8	M(A)
Davenham	1946	285	98	23	8	M(A)
Frances Poole	1923	175	96	22	8	M(A)
Hibernia	1897	128	85	20	7	M(A)
John Calderwood	1913	147	86	21	7½	M(A)
Jubilee	1904	136	85	21	7½	M(A)
Oswald	1915	191	97	22	8	M(A)
Seaforth Trader* ex Capricorn-72, Olivier van Noort-70	1952	480	169	28	10	M(A)
Weaverham	1948	201	103	22	8	M(A)
Wincham	1948	201	103	22	8	M(A)
New (3)	1974/75	1,000 dw	139	26	9¾	M(2)(A)

See also Tugs

BURIES MARKES LTD

London

FUNNEL: Black with blue letters "BM" on broad white band between narrow red bands.
HULL: Black with red boot-topping.

Name	Built	Tons	Length	Breadth	Speed	Engines
Coastal Chemical Tankers:						
La Hacienda	1969	1,452	264	42	13	M(A)
La Quinta	1969	1,452	264	42	13	M(A)

BURRY SAND CO LTD

Llanelly

FUNNEL: Red with black top and yellow letters "BSC" in yellow ring.
HULL: Black.

Name	Built	Tons	Length	Breadth	Speed	Engines
Sand Dredger and Carrier:						
Coedmor ex Arran Monarch-64, Vic 57-48	1946	181	108	20	9	M(A)
Tankard X8	1915	134	106	22	7	M(A)

CALEDONIAN-Mac BRAYNE LTD
(Scottish Transport Group)

Glasgow

FUNNEL: Red with black top and red Scottish lion on yellow disc.
HULL: Black with red boot-topping and white line or blue with red boot-topping.

Name	Built	Tons	Length	Breadth	Speed	Engines
Car and Passenger Ferries:						

Caledonian-Mac Brayne Ltd (Continued)

Name	Built	Tons	Length	Breadth	Speed	Engines
Arran	1953	568	186	36	15	M(2)
Bute	1954	568	186	36	15	M(2)
Caledonia	1966	1,156	203	41	15	M(2)
ex Stena Baltica-69						
Clansman	1964	1,420	265	46	14½	M
Claymore	1955	1,021	192	38	12½	M
Cowall	1954	569	186	36	15	M(2)
Glen Sannox	1957	1,107	257	46	17	M(2)
Iona	1970	1,192	245	46	12½	M
Jupiter	1974	980	227	45	15½	M(2)(A)
Juno	1974	849	227	45	15½	M(2)(A)
King George V	1926	985	270	32	16	ST(2)
Kyleakin	1970	225	161	42	8	M(2)
Loch Arkaig	1942	179	113	22	10	M(2)
Loch Carron	1951	683	203	34	11	M(A)
Maid of Cumbrae	1953	508	165	30	14	M(2)
Queen Mary II	1933	1,014	263	35	19	ST(3)
Caledonian MacBrayne Holdings Ltd:						
Columba	1964	1,420	265	46	14	M
Hebrides	1964	1,420	265	46	14½	M
Pioneer	1974	1,080			16	M
Suilven	1974	1,870			16	M(2)
Paddle Steamer Preservation Society:						
Waverley	1947	693	240	57	14	SR(PW)
Loch Lomond Service:						
Maid of the Loch	1953	555	208	51	12	SR(PW)

CARISBROOKE SHIPPING LTD

Newport, I.O.W.

FUNNEL: Yellow with black "CW" monogram in black ring.
HULL: Grey with black boot-topping.

Name	Built	Tons	Length	Breadth	Speed	Engines
Greta C.	1963	451	170	24	9	M(A)
ex Westland Trader-72						

The Company employ foreign flag tonnage on charter

CARTER & WARD OF WICKFORD LTD

Wickford

FUNNEL: Black with red top separated by white band.
HULL: Black.

Name	Built	Tons	Length	Breadth	Speed	Engines
Sand Dredgers and Carriers:						
Careyna ex Constellation-68, Comity-64, C. 648-58	1949	211	105	22	8	M(A)

CAWOODS FUELS (N.I.) LTD
(Cawood Holdings Ltd)

Belfast

FUNNEL: Yellow with black top and Cawood Wharton monogram in black inside black ring.
HULL: Black with red boot-topping.

Name	Built	Tons	Length	Breadth	Speed	Engines
Craigmore	1965	1,359	240	37	11	M(A)

CENTRAL ELECTRICITY GENERATING BOARD

London

FUNNEL: Red with black top and black rings.
HULL: Black with white top line and red boot-topping.

Name	Built	Tons	Length	Breadth	Speed	Engines
Charles H. Merz	1955	2,947	340	43	11½	SR(A)
Cliff Quay	1950	3,345	339	46	10½	SR(A)
James Rowan	1955	2,947	340	44	11¼	SR(A)
Sir John Snell	1955	2,947	340	47	11	SR(A)
Sir Johnstone Wright	1955	3,382	339	47	11	SR(A)
Sir William Walker	1954 ✓	2,901	340	44	11¼	SR(A)

Name	Built	Tons	Length	Breadth	Speed	Engines
Thames "Up-River" or "Flatiron" colliers:						
Battersea	1951	1,777	271	40	11	M(A)
Blackwall Point	1951	1,776	271	40	11	M(A)
Dame Caroline Haslett*	1950	1,777	271	40	11	M(A)
Harry Richardson	1950	1,777	271	40	11	M(A)
Hopper Barges:						
Bessie Surtees	1955	561	158	33	10¾	M(A)
Sir Fon	1950	814	185	36	11¼	M(A)

* *Fitted for cable-laying 1974.*

CHANNEL ISLAND FERRIES LTD

Guernsey

FUNNEL: Yellow.
HULL: White.

Name	Built	Tons	Length	Breadth	Speed	Engines
Ferry:						
Fleur des Iles	1973	681	155	39	13½	M(2)(A)

CHARRINGTON TANKERS LTD

London

FUNNEL: Yellow with black top and broad blue band between narrow white bands.
HULL: Black with red boot-topping.

Name	Built	Tons	Length	Breadth	Speed	Engines
Thames Tankers:						
Charcrest ✓	1964	465	163	34	8¾	M(A)
Charmo ✓	1960	477	163	34	10	M(A)

CITY & COUNTY OF THE CITY OF EXETER

Exeter

FUNNEL: Black with City crest in full colour.
HULL: Grey with red boot-topping.

Name	Built	Tons	Length	Breadth	Speed	Engines
Sludge Carrier:						
S.W.2	1963	256	123	25	8½	M(A)

CIVIL & MARINE LTD

London

FUNNEL: Red with black top separated by narrow white band and white letters "CM".
HULL: Black with red boot-topping.

Name	Built	Tons	Length	Breadth	Speed	Engines
Sand Dredgers and Carriers:						
Cambrae ✓	1973	3,750	333	56	12	M(A)
Cambrook ✓	1967	1,574	250	54	11½	M(A)
Paterna	1915	154	105	21	7	M(A)
ex Helen Birch–51, Studland						

CLYDE SHIPPING CO LTD

Glasgow

FUNNEL: Black.
HULL: Black with red boot-topping.

Name	Built	Tons	Length	Breadth	Speed	Engines
Toward	1960	1,323	230	35	11½	M(A)
ex Yewglen–74, Tolsta–70						

Chartered to Glenlight Shipping Ltd

C.M.S. (SHIPPING) LTD

London

FUNNEL: Orange with white letters "CMS" on red bordered blue panel.
HULL:

Name	Built	Tons	Length	Breadth	Speed	Engines
Molar Venture✓	1972	597	189	33	11	M(A)

COASTAL MOTORSHIPS LTD

Wallasay

FUNNEL: Red with black chevron top.
HULL: Light green with dark green boot-topping.

Name	Built	Tons	Length	Breadth	Speed	Engines
Lorraine D. ex Cambrian Coast-71, Launched as Jan T.	1957	560	187	30	10	M(A)

S. WILLIAMS COE & CO LTD
(Booker McConnell Ltd)

Liverpool

FUNNEL: Blue with blue letter "C" on white band.
HULL: Grey or black with red or green boot-topping.

Name	Built	Tons	Length	Breadth	Speed	Engines
Blackthorn	1960	749	190	34	11	M(A)
Briarthorn* ex Anne-73, Anne Bogelund- 69	1968	1,503	264	39	12	M(A)
Maythorn	1962	771	190	35	11	M(A)

* Fitted for drilling platform and mooring anchors

Top: CHARLES H. MERZ, Central Electricity Generating Board *F. R. Sherlock*

CARDA QUEEN, Comfin (Commodity & Finance) Co Ltd *F. R. Sherlock*

S. Williams Coe & Co Ltd (Continued)

Name	Built	Tons	Length	Breadth	Speed	Engines
Rosethorn ex Yewkyle-74, Laksa-71	1960	1,323	230	35	11½	M(A)
Silverthorn ex Yewhill-74	1957	1,089	221	35	10½	M(A)
Quickthorn ex Tanmarack-73	1967	1,596	280	42	13	M(A)
Whitethorn† ex Hero-70	1963	1,513	261	40	14	M(A)
Thorn Line Finance Ltd:						
Firethorn √	1963	1,041	220	38	12	M(A)

† Fitted with drilling platform and mooring anchors, on charter to N.E.R.C.
See also Metcalfe Motor Coasters Ltd

COLCHESTER SHIPPING CO
Tiptree, Essex
FUNNEL: Yellow with black top.
HULL: Black.

Name	Built	Tons	Length	Breadth	Speed	Enines
Mary Birch ex Swanage-35, ex Admiralty X- Lighter	1915	157	106	21	6½	M(A)
P. R. Banyard:						
Carita	1913	140	96	26	7½	M(A)

COMFIN (COMMODITY & FINANCE) CO LTD
London
FUNNEL: Blue with blue letter "C" on white diamond or yellow letter "C" on yellow bordered blue diamond.
HULL: Green or grey with red boot-topping.

Name	Built	Tons	Length	Breadth	Speed	Engines
Carda Knight ex Anna Lüehmann-74, Anna Lühmann-72, Karin Lüdke-70	1966	999	230	33	11½	M(A)

Comfin (Commodity & Finance) Co Ltd (Continued)

Name	Built	Tons	Length	Breadth	Speed	Engines
Carda Princess ex Hardy Merchant-73	1964	469	165	28	10	M(A)
Carda Queen ex Schleswig- Hostein-73	1964	499	196	33	10½	M(A)

COMMODORE SHIPPING CO LTD

Guernsey, C.I.

FUNNEL: Blue with golden or yellow lion device.
HULL: Black with white line and green boot-topping.

Name	Built	Tons	Length	Breadth	Speed	Engines
Commodore Clipper ex Mayo-74, Hibernian Enterprise-71	1970	758	257	39	15	M(A)
Commodore Goodwill ex Goodwill-68	1958	499	196	33	12½	M(A)
Commodore Transporters Ltd:						
Commodore Trader	1971	477	162	29	10¼	M(A)
Island Commodore	1971	496	227	36	12½	M(A)
Norman Commodore	1971	496	226	36	12	M(A)

D. COOK LTD

Hull

FUNNEL: Red with black top.
HULL: Black.

Name	Built	Tons	Length	Breadth	Speed	Engines
Humber Tankers:						
Onward Pioneer	1955	164	122	19	8	M(A)
S. T. Morgan ex Admiralty X-Lighter	1915	139	106	21	7	M(A)

WILLIAM COOPER & SONS LTD
(Ready Mix Group)

Widnes & Feltham, Middx.

FUNNEL: Yellow with black top or orange with black letter 'C'.
HULL: Grey with black boot-topping.

Name	Built	Tons	Length	Breadth	Speed	Engines
Sand Dredgers and Carriers:						
William Cooper	1965	553	157	34	9½	M(A)
J. Henry Schroder Wagg & Co Ltd:						
Raynestone ex Maple-74, Malta Faith-72, Soutra-69	1958	1,334	229	35	11½	M(A)

See also Hall Dredging Ltd

DAVID COPESTAKE

London

FUNNEL: Black with red over black over red bands.
HULL: Grey with black boot-topping.

Name	Built	Tons	Length	Breadth	Speed	Engines
Citadel	1950	376	138	25	9	M(A)

CORNISH SHIPPING CO LTD
(Harris & Co (Shipping) Ltd)

Par

FUNNEL: Blue with white "CS" monogram.
HULL: Dark grey with black boot-topping.

Name	Built	Tons	Length	Breadth	Speed	Engines
Flint ex Gisela Flint-74	1961	300	155	28	10	M(A)

Cornish Shipping Co Ltd (Continued)

Name	Built	Tons	Length	Breadth	Speed	Engines
Polkerris ex Osterbrucke- 72, Hein Shur- 68	1958	294	156	27	9½	M(A)
Vauban	1962	370	148	24	10	M(A)

CORONET SHIPPING CO LTD

London

FUNNEL: Green with black or green letters "CS" on white band.
HULL: Grey with red boot-topping.

Name	Built	Tons	Length	Breadth	Speed	Engines
Narya	1971	1,594	278	43	12½	M(A)
Nanya	1971	1,594	278	43	12½	M(A)
Vilya	1971	1,594	278	43	12½	M(A)
New (2)	1976	3,100 dw			13	M(A)

Wm. CORY & SON LTD
(A division of Ocean Transport & Trading Ltd.)

London

FUNNEL: Black with black diamond on broad white band.
HULL: Black or grey with or without white line and red boot-topping.

Name	Built	Tons	Length	Breadth	Speed	Engines
Cory Maritime Ltd:						
Oil/Chemical *Tankers:*						
Cordale*	1970	918	231	32	11	M(A)

* *Vessels incorporated in the fleet of Panocean Shipping & Terminals Ltd*

Wm Cory & Son Ltd (Continued)

Name	Built	Tons	Length	Breadth	Speed	Engines
Cordene* Pass of	1970	918	231	32	11	M(A)
Balmaha* Pass of	1974	1,600			12	M(A)
Brander* Pass of	1974	1,600			12	M(A)
Drumochte* Pass of	1974	1,600			12	M(A)
Glenclunie*√	1963	1,416	245	38	11½	M(A)
New*	1975	1,600			12	M(A)
Cory Tank Craft Ltd:						
Thames Tankers:						
Battle Stone	1968	293	130	27	8	M(A)
Bruce Stone	1964	357	143	30	11	M(A)
Druid Stone	1967	236	119	26	7½	M(A)
London Stone	1957	438	155	31	11	M(A)
Rebus Stone	1963	177	115	26	8	M(A)
Rufus Stone	1963	165	115	26	8	M(A)
Wade Stone	1968	180	115	26	7½	M(A)
Liquid Gas Tankers Ltd:						
Corbank	1956	2,059	305	40	12	M(A)
Corchester	1965	4,840	370	53	12	M(A)
South Coast Shipping Co Ltd:						
Sand Dredgers and Carriers:						
Sand Finch ex Ron Woolaway-70, Selskar-60	1958	478	165	27	10	M(A)
Sand Gull	1964	534	174	30	9½	M(A)
Sand Lark	1963	540	174	30	9½	M(A)
Sand Skua	1971	1,168	218	41	9½	M(A)
Sand Snipe	1961	517	174	30	9½	M(A)
Sand Swan	1969	1,164	218	41	9½	M(A)
Sand Swift	1969	1,085	218	41	9½	M(A)
Sand Tern	1964	535	174	30	9	M(A)
Sand Weaver √	1974	3,100	316	56	10	M(A)
New	1974	1,168	218	41	9½	M(A)

See also Tug Section

* *Vessels incorporated in the fleet of Panocean Shipping & Terminals Ltd*

CROSON LTD

(H. J. Bolson)

Poole

FUNNEL: Yellow with black top with black letter "C" on black bordered white diamond superimposed on yellow over red over broad yellow over blue bands.
HULL: Blue or white with red boot-topping.

Name	Built	Tons	Length	Breadth	Speed	Engines
Bournemouth & Poole area Excursion Vessels:						
Bournemouth Queen ex Coronia-68	1935	227	130	26	11	M(2)
Poole Belle ex Matapan-68, ex M.L.	1941	127	107	18	10	M(2)
Swanage Queen ex Thornwick-68	1938	128	98	21	10	M
Wessex Belle ex Swanage Belle-68	1942	121	106	18	10	M(2)

W. G. S. CROUCH & SONS LTD

Greenhithe

FUNNEL: Yellow with blue over white over red over white over blue bands.
HULL: Black.

Name	Built	Tons	Length	Breadth	Speed	Engines
Fresh Water/Estuaral Tankers:						
Harriet Spearing ex Stourgate-63	1924	115	90	19	7	M(A)
William Spearing ex Apexity-65	1945	136	100	20	8	M(A)

See also Tugs

R. CUNNINGHAM (SCALPAY) CO LTD
(R. Cameron & Co Ltd)

Stornoway

FUNNEL: Yellow with black top and white over blue over red bands.
HULL: Grey with black boot-topping.

Name	Built	Tons	Length	Breadth	Speed	Engines
Eilean Glas ex Th'Eilean Glas-72, Ceres- 71, Overysel-68	1961	374	156	25	10	M(A)
Ocean Hunter ex Caledonian- 71	1961	127	84	23	11½	M

THE DENHOLM LINE STEAMERS LTD
Glasgow

FUNNEL:
HULL:

Name	Built	Tons	Length	Breadth	Speed	Engines
Monach ex Mornes-74	1972	1,594	262	45	12¾	M(A)

ONESIMUS DOREY (1972) LTD
Guernsey, C.I.

FUNNEL: Black with blue letter "D" on white diamond on red square interrupting blue band.
HULL: Black with red boot-topping.

Name	Built	Tons	Length	Breadth	Speed	Engines
Havelet	1964	1,042	217	34	11½	M(A)
Perelle ex Kinnaird Head-72	1963	1,985	290	42	12½	M(A)
Portelet	1961	1,042	217	34	11½	M(A)

W. E. DOWDS LTD

Newport, Mon.

FUNNEL: Green with black top.
HULL: Black with red boot-topping.

Name	Built	Tons	Length	Breadth	Speed	Engines
Brandon	1957	586	170	29	9	M(A)
Colston	1955	586	170	29	9	M(A)

G. DUPENOIS SHIPPING CO LTD

Poundsgate, Devon

FUNNEL: Black with three orange bands interrupted by white "GD"
monogram.
HULL: Black with red boot-topping.

Name	Built	Tons	Length	Breadth	Speed	Engines
Grete Krönke ex Teun-66	1952	500	187	29	10	M(A)

EARNBANK SAND & GRAVEL CO LTD
(D. & R. Taylor Ltd)

Perth

FUNNEL: Blue with broad silver band.
HULL: Black.

Name	Built	Tons	Length	Breadth	Speed	Engines
Sand Dredgers and Carriers:						
Severn Merchant	1936	122	92	19	7½	M(A)
Rayjohn	1931	155	105	22	7	M(A)
(Unnamed) ex Antiquity-66	1933	311	129	25	9	M(A)

EFFLUENT HANDLING LTD

Belfast

FUNNEL: None.
HULL: Black.

Name	Built	Tons	Length	Breadth	Speed	Engines
Southdale H.	1951	298	152	22	9	M(A)

EFFLUENTS SERVICES LTD

Macclesfield

FUNNEL: Green with black letters "ESL" on white band.
HULL: Grey or black with red boot-topping.

Name	Built	Tons	Length	Breadth	Speed	Enjnes
Coastal Effluent Tankers:						
Errwood ex Ramaga-73, Marine Fairway-72, Capcos Lupe-70, Cap Cos-67	1950	471	186	26	9½	M(A)
Kinder ex Anthony M.-70, Empire Tigity-47, Göhren-45	1944	465	159	26	9	M(A)
Kindill	1955	778	198	33	10½	M(A)
Marine Seaway ex Bridgeman-69, Tripp-50	1939	369	154	26	8½	M(A)
Scamonden ex Florencestan-73, Thorwald-68, Vigilanter-55, Noord-55	1949	582	199	28	8	M(A)

EGGAR, FORRESTER (HOLDINGS) LTD

London

FUNNEL: Pale blue with dark blue stag head device.
HULL: Grey with red boot-topping.

Name	Built	Tons	Length	Breadth	Speed	Engines
Wib	1970	199	137	25	9	M(A)
Wiggs	1970	199	137	25	9	M(A)
Wopper	1968	260	137	25	9½	M(A)
ex Continent-70						
Eggar Forrester Ltd:						
Wilks	1969	199	137	25	9	M(A)
Wis	1970	199	137	25	9	M(A)

ELDER DEMPSTER LINES LTD
(Ocean Transport & Trading Ltd)

Liverpool

FUNNEL: Yellow.
HULL: Black with red boot-topping.

Name	Built	Tons	Length	Breadth	Speed	Engines
Car & Vehicle Carrier:						
Clearway	1970	1,160	300	55	15	M(A)
ex Speedway-70						

ELLERMAN LINES LTD
(Ellerman Group—Shipping Division)

London & Hull

FUNNEL: Red with black top.
HULL: Dark green with red boot-topping, or grey with red boot-topping.

Name	Built	Tons	Length	Breadth	Speed	Engines
Destro	1970	1,571	360	64	17	M(2)(A)
Rapallo	1960	3,402	366	54	13½	M

Ellerman Lines Ltd (Continued)

Name	Built	Tons	Length	Breadth	Speed	Engines
Salerno	1965	1,559	308	46	13	M(A)
Salmo	1967	1,523	308	46	13	M(A)
Sangro	1968	1,523	308	46	13	M(A)
Silvio	1968	1,523	308	46	13	M(A)
Sorrento	1967	1,523	308	46	13	M(A)
Domino Container Ships Ltd:						
Domino	1971	1,582	356	64	17	M(2)(A)
Domino Container Ships & Det Forende D/S:						
Car and Vehicle Ferry:						
Hero	1972	3,375	376	69	17	M(2)(A)
Department of Trade & Industry:						
Fishery Mother and Weather Ship:						
Miranda ex Dorothea-71, Donna-69, Albatross-67	1942	1,462	235	38	11½	M(A)

ELWICK BAY SHIPPING CO LTD

Stromness

FUNNEL: Blue or blue with two horizontal yellow bars.
HULL: Black with red boot-topping.

Name	Built	Tons	Length	Breadth	Speed	Engines
Elwick Bay ex Torwood-59, Plympton-48, Dartmeet-47, Norrix-46, Ellen M.-36	1930	262	122	23	9	M(A)
Inganess Bay ex Traly-73, Weisser Grief-72, Regulus-62	1950	298	145	24	10	M(A)

ESSO PETROLEUM CO LTD

London

FUNNEL: Black with red "Esso" in blue ring on broad white band.
HULL: Black or grey with red boot-topping.

Name	Built	Tons	Length	Breadth	Speed	Engines
Coastal Tankers:						
Esso Brixham	1957	758	196	34	10	M(A)
Esso Caernarvon	1962	1,103	231	36	10	M(A)
Esso Clyde†	1972	12,317	546	75	15½	M(A)
Esso Dover	1961	490	176	27	10	M(A)
Esso Fawley†	1967	11,064	534	72	16¾	M(A) 2in
Esso Hythe	1959	856	209	35	10	M(A)
Esso Inverness	1971	2,178	300	42	13	M(A)
Esso Ipswich	1960	1,103	231	36	9½	M(A)
Esso Lyndhurst	1958	856	209	35	10	M(A)
Esso Mersey†	1972	12,323	546	75	15½	M(A)
Esso Milford Haven† ✓	1968	11,046	354	72	16¾	M(A)
Esso Penzance	1971	2,178	300	42	13	M(A)
Esso Preston*	1956	1,965	299	42	10½	SR(A)
Esso Purfleet	1967	2,838	324	47	12	M(A)
Esso Tenby	1971	2,170	300	42	13½	M(A)
Esso Tynemouth	1960	501	171	28	9½	M(A)
Esso Woolston	1958	856	210	35	10	M(A)
New	1974	20,400dw			15½	M(A)

* Bitumen Tanker
† Esso Clyde, Esso Fawley, Esso Mersey and Esso Milford Haven were built for coastal use

F. T. EVERARD & SONS LTD

London

FUNNEL: Black, or grey, or yellow, with red and white diagonally quartered houseflag.
HULL: Black with white topline and red boot-topping; Yellow with red or green boot-topping; Blue-grey or grey with red or black boot-topping.

Name	Built	Tons	Length	Breadth	Speed	Engines
Ability	1943	881	203	30	10	M(A)
Actuality	1966	698	224	35	11	M(A)
Apricity	1967	692	224	35	11	M(A)
Centricity	1955	655	191	28	10	M(A)
Centurity	1956	770	204	30	10	M(A)
Continuity	1955	655	191	28	10	M(A)
Ethel Everard ✓	1966	1,599	279	41	10	M(A)

F. T. Everard & Sons Ltd (Continued)

Name	Built	Tons	Length	Breadth	Speed	Engines
Fixity	1966	200	117	25	9	M(A)
Formality	1968	200	117	25	9	M(A)
Fred Everard	1972	1,600	299	44	12¾	M(A)
Frivolity	1963	199	110	25	8	M(A)
Georgina V. Everard	1955	2,487	306	42	10	M(A)
Mairi Everard	1974	1,599	299	44	12¾	M(A)
Penelope Everard	1963	1,583	265	39	11	M(A)
Rosemary Everard ✔	1965	1,599	266	39	11	M(A)
Sagacity	1973	1,595	299	44	12½	M(A)
Sanguity	1956	1,543	241	38	10½	M(A)
Security	1971	1,596	279	42	12½	M(A)
Selectivity	1952	1,575	241	38	10½	M(A)
Serenity	1970	1,597	279	42	12½	M(A)
Severity	1954	590	184	28	10	M(A)
Similarity	1951	1,575	241	38	10½	M(A)
Sincerity	1971	1,598	279	42	12½	M(A)
Sonority	1952	589	184	28	11	M(A)
Suavity	1972	1,595	299	44	12¾	M(A)
Summity	1972	1,595	299	44	12¾	M(A)
Superiority	1972	1,597	284	42	12½	M(A)
New (2)	1975	900dw			10	M(A)
Coastal Tankers:						
Acclivity	1968	299	168	28	10	M(A)
Activity	1969	698	243	34	12	M(A)
Agility	1959	1,016	214	35	11	M(A)
Alacrity	1966	943	216	35	12	M(A)
Allurity ✔	1969	698	243	34	12	M(A)
Annuity	1961	1,600	266	40	10	M(A)
Assiduity	1964	1,249	234	36	11	M(A)
Audacity	1968	699	238	36	11½	M(A)
Authority	1966	500	215	33	12	M(A)
Clydesdale Shipowners Co Ltd:						
Gillian Everard	1963	1,598	266	39	11	M(A)
Grit	1966	498	220	34	12½	M(A)
ex Dagmar Stenhoj-70						
Coastal Tanker:						
Asperity	1967	698	236	32	12	M(A)
Everard Shipping Co Ltd:						
Capacity	1963	461	170	28	9	M(A)
Clarity	1957	764	204	30	10	M(A)

F. T. Everard & Sons Ltd (Continued)

Name	Built	Tons	Length	Breadth	Speed	Engines
J. Hay & Sons Ltd:						
Alfred Everard	1957	1,543	241	38	10	M(A)
Futurity	1968	198	110	25	9	M(A)
The Duchess	1963	461	170	28	9	M(A)
Scottish Navigation Co Ltd						
Supremity	1970	698	265	45	13½	M(A)
Thames Tankers Ltd:						
Coastal Tankers:						
Amity ex Thuntank 5-72	1969	2,901	323	47	12¾	M(A)
Anteriority ex Thuntank 6-72	1969	2,901	323	47	12¾	M(A)

See also Tugs

EVERETT SHIPPING & TRADING CO LTD

Ingatestone & Dagenham, Essex

FUNNEL: White with black top and yellow letter "E" on broad blue band.
HULL: Grey or black with red boot-topping.

Name	Built	Tons	Length	Breadth	Speed	Engines
Biscaya	1957	494	203	31	10	M(A)
Fair Jennifer ex Westminster- brook-73	1961	1,103	217	34	11	M(A)

FIFE SHIPPING CO LTD

London

FUNNEL: Yellow.
HULL: Green with brown boot-topping.

Name	Built	Tons	Length	Breadth	Speed	Engines
D. Cumming & Co Ltd\ London,						
Joan C. ex Antilla-70	1957	526	185	29	10	M(A)
G. E. French, Frinton-on-Sea:						
Gena F. ex Deo Duce-72	1957	500	190	29	11	M(A)
Henry W. Peabody Grain Ltd, London:						
Lovat ex Avant-73, Skive-68	1962	1,118	221	35	11	M(A)
Mrs N. V. Williamson & Mrs Y. Andrews, London:						
Jointyn ex Juvalta-73	1959	499	186	30	10	M(A)

JAMES FISHER & SONS LTD

Barrow

FUNNEL: Yellow with black top and black letter "F" on broad white band over narrow black band.
HULL: Black with yellow line and red boot-topping.

Name	Built	Tons	Length	Breadth	Speed	Engines
Aberthaw Fisher* ✔	1966	2,355	276	54	11¾	M
Brathay Fisher	1971	2,109	348	55	14½	M(A)
Derwent Fisher	1966	1,096	217	34	12	M(A)
Eden Fisher	1965	1,173	237	35	11	M(A)
Guernsey Fisher†	1971	829	270	40	12½	M(A)
Jersey Fisher†	1971	829	270	40	12½	M(A)
Kingsnorth Fisher*	1966	2,355	275	54	11¾	M
Leven Fisher	1962	1,540	260	39	12½	M(A)
Orwell Fisher	1968	1,374	296	50	14½	M(A)

Top: FRED EVERARD, F. T. Everard & Sons Ltd *Charles A. Hill*

ONWARD MARINER, Fleetwood Tankers Ltd *J. K. Byass*

James Fisher & Sons Ltd (Continued)

Name	Built	Tons	Length	Breadth	Speed	Engines
Pool Fisher	1959	1,028	218	34	11	M(A)
Solway Fisher	1968	1,374	296	50	14½	M(A)
Anchorage Ferrying Services Ltd:						
Odin	1968	1,844	242	41	9	M(2)(A)
Seaway Coasters Ltd:						
Lune Fisher	1962	1,012	218	34	12½	M(A)

* *Strengthened for heavy Ro-Ro cargo over stern ramp & chartered to C.E.G.B.*

† *Chartered to British Rail and operating in their colours*

JOSEPH FISHER & SONS LTD
(Cawood Holdings Ltd)

Newry

FUNNEL: Black with red over white over blue bands.
HULL: Black with red boot-topping.

Name	Built	Tons	Length	Breadth	Speed	Engines
Olive	1963	791	202	33	11	M(A)

FLEETWOOD SAND & GRAVEL CO LTD

Fleetwood

FUNNEL: Black with yellow over blue over yellow bands.
HULL: Black with red boot-topping.

Name	Built	Tons	Length	Breadth	Speed	Engines
Sand Dredgers and Carriers:						
Pen Itchen ex Ben Hebden	1947	399	145	25	8	M(A)

FLEETWOOD TANKERS LTD

(Boston Group Holdings Ltd)

Fleetwood

FUNNEL: Red with black top.
HULL: Black with red boot-topping.

Name	Built	Tons	Length	Breadth	Speed	Engines
Coastal Tankers:						
Beckton ✓ launched as Onward Voyager	1971	239	132	22	8½	M(A)
Onward Mariner	1970	239	131	22	8½	M(A)

See also Hull Gates Shipping Co Ltd

FORUMCASTLE LTD

Westcliffe-on-Sea

FUNNEL: Dark blue.
HULL: Grey with black boot-topping.

Name	Built	Tons	Length	Breadth	Speed	Engines
Nimrod	1948	378	162	27	9	M(A)

FOX ELMS LTD

Gloucester

FUNNEL: Black.
HULL: Black.

Name	Built	Tons	Length	Breadth	Speed	Engines
Severn Trader	1932	119	89	19	7½	M(A)

Wm. FRANCE, FENWICK & CO LTD
(Houlder Brothers & Co Ltd)

London

FUNNEL: Black with red letters "FF" on broad white band.
HULL: Black with red boot-topping.

Name	Built	Tons	Length	Breadth	Speed	Engines
Chelwood	1964	5,440	370	54	13	M(A)

FRANCIS CONCRETE LTD
(Marine Aggregate Div)

Chichester

FUNNEL: Green with narrow black top and "FRANCIS" in white.
HULL: Grey with green boot-topping.

Name	Built	Tons	Length	Breadth	Speed	Engines
Sand Dredger and Carrier:						
Chichester City	1971	991	196	39	10	M(A)
Chichester Gem	1970	1,579	252	46	12	M(A)
ex Pen Stour-74						
Chichester Star	1973	986	196	39	10	M(A)

FREIGHT EXPRESS—SEACON LTD

London

FUNNEL: Black with blue and yellow chequered panel.
HULL: Grey with green boot-topping.

Name	Built	Tons	Length	Breadth	Speed	Engines
Cornish Chieftain†	1955	2,122	281	40	$12\frac{1}{2}$	M(A)
ex Realengracht -74, Burstah-70						
Sea Ems*	1956	389	161	26	$9\frac{1}{2}$	M(A)
ex Barbara J-73, Helena-68						
Sea Maas*	1973	499	176	32	$11\frac{1}{2}$	M(A)
Sea Rhine	1970	198	147	24	10	M(A)
Sea Thames*	1973	499	176	32	$11\frac{1}{2}$	M(A)

* *Singapore flag*
† *Demise chartered to Iffie Corineus Lines Ltd.*

EAGLE, Southern Ferries Ltd *F. R. Sherlock*

GALLIC ESTATES LTD

London

FUNNEL: Blue with narrow wavy blue band on broad white band.
HULL: Dark grey with red boot-topping.

Name	Built	Tons	Length	Breadth	Speed	Engines
Gallic Minch ex Tornes-74	1971	1,589	262	45	12½	M(A)
Gallic Stream ex Fonnes-74	1971	1,594	262	45	12½	M(A)

J. & A. GARDNER LTD

Glasgow

FUNNEL: Black with white band.
HULL: Black with white line and green boot-topping, or grey with green or black boot-topping.

Name	Built	Tons	Length	Breadth	Speed	Engines
Saint Aidan	1962	973	218	34	12	M(A)
Saint Angus ex Milo-69	1953	991	224	34	11½	M(A)
Saint Bedan	1972	1,251	237	38	12	M(A)
Saint Colman	1963	975	205	33	12	M(A)
Saint Enoch ex Yorkshire Coast-72	1959	785	196	33	11	M(A)
Saint Fergus	1964	346	143	27	10½	M(A)
Saint Kentigern*	1973	460	167	29	10½	M(A)
Saint Modan	1960	480	166	27	12	M(A)
Saint Ronan	1966	433	147	28	12	M(A)
Saint William	1967	781	204	32	12	M(A)

* *Bow ramp, self discharging (3T crane), hatch strengthened (120 tons)*

GENERAL STEAM NAVIGATION (TRADING) LTD
(Peninsular & Oriental Short Sea Shipping Ltd)
(P & O Group)

London

FUNNEL: Black with houseflag (White with red globe surmounting date "1824" in centre with red letters "GSNC" in each corner.
HULL: Black with white line and red boot-topping.

Name	Built	Tons	Length	Breadth	Speed	Engines
Albatross	1965	654	214	36	13	M(A)
Avocet	1965	654	214	36	13	M(A)
Dorset Coast	1959	1,225	220	36	11½	M(A)
Oriole	1963	430	149	28	10	M(A)
Ortolan	1964	430	149	28	10	M(A)
Petrel	1965	496	160	29	12	M(A)

Normandy Ferries Ltd: (Southern Ferries Ltd & S.A.G.A. Paris) (Funnel: Pale blue with black top and houseflag; Hull: White with red boot-topping)

Car and Vehicle Ferries:

Dragon	1967	5,720	440	72	19	M(2)
Leopard*	1968	6,014	442	72	19	M(2)

Southern Ferries Ltd: (Funnel: Pale blue with yellow eagle on white shield and black top; Hull: White with red boot-topping)

Car and Vehicle Ferries:

Eagle	1971	11,609	466	74	23	M(2)(A)
SF Panther	1965	4,407	404	61	20	M(2)
ex Peter Pan-73						

* French flag

See also Belfast Steamship Co Ltd, North of Scotland Orkney & Shetland Shipping Co Ltd, North Sea Ferries Ltd and Tyne-Tees Steam Shipping Co Ltd

Geo. GIBSON & CO LTD
(Runcimen Group)

Edinburgh

FUNNEL: Black or those of charterer.
HULL: Black with red boot-topping or red.

Name	Built	Tons	Length	Breadth	Speed	Engines
Coastal Liquefied Gas/Chemical Tankers:						

Geo. Gibson & Co Ltd (Continued)

Name	Built	Tons	Length	Breadth	Speed	Engines
Anchor Gas Tankers Ltd:						
Dryburgh	1952	1,593	261	38	11¾	M(A)
Lanrick	1957	1,177	244	36	12½	M(A)
Quentin	1940	574	174	28	10½	M(A)
Gibson Gas Tankers Ltd:						
Heriot	1972	1,584	256	42	14½	M(A)
Melrose	1971	1,999	285	43	14	M(A)
Liquid Gas Equipment Ltd:						
Abbotsford	1972	1,584	258	42	14½	M(A)
Nile Steamship Co Ltd:						
Teviot	1966	694	186	33	11½	M(A)
Ship Mortgage Finance Co Ltd:						
Traquair	1966	694	186	33	11½	M(A)
Deutsche Geo. Gibson & Co Gastanker GmbH (Singapore flag):						
Bucklaw	1972	972	216	34	11	M(A)
Durward	1971	844	183	33	11	M(A)

G. T. GILLIE & BLAIR LTD

Newcastle

FUNNEL : Black with broad blue band between narrow white bands.
HULL : Black with red boot-topping separated by a white line.

Name	Built	Tons	Length	Breadth	Speed	Engines
Firth Shipping Co Ltd:						
Moray Firth IV	1960	613	182	29	10½	M(A)
Tilling Construction Services Ltd—TILCON:						
New	1974	780	203	33	12	M(A)
Olna Firth	1957	591	176	29	10¾	M(A)

GLASGOW CORPORATION

Glasgow

FUNNEL: Yellow with black top.
HULL: Pale grey with red boot-topping.

Name	Built	Tons	Length	Breadth	Speed	Engines
Sludge Carriers:						
Dalmarnock	1970	2,266	313	51	11	M(A)
Shieldhall	1955	1,792	268	45	11	SR(A)

R. D. GLEESON (DERBY) LTD

Derby

FUNNEL:
HULL: Black.

Name	Built	Tons	Length	Breadth	Speed	Engines
Effluent Tanker:						
Wheeldale H.	1953	273	141	22	8	M(A)

GLENLIGHT SHIPPING LTD

Glasgow

FUNNEL: Dark red with black top.
HULL: Black with red boot-topping.

Name	Built	Tons	Length	Breadth	Speed	Engines
Dawnlight I	1965	199	107	22	$9\frac{1}{2}$	M(A)
Glencloy	1966	200	109	24	9	M(A)
Glenfyne	1965	200	109	24	9	M(A)
Pibroch	1957	157	87	20	$9\frac{1}{2}$	M(A)

Glenlight Shipping Ltd (Continued)

Name	Built	Tons	Length	Breadth	Speed	Engines
Light Shipping Co Ltd:						
Fairlight	1966	200	109	24	9	M(A)
Raylight	1963	177	97	21	9	M(A)

GOMBA SHIPPING LTD

London

FUNNEL: Green with black top separated by red band bearing white letter 'G'.
HULL: Black with red boot-topping.

Name	Built	Tons	Length	Breadth	Speed	Engines
Gomba Enterprise ex Richmond Queen-74, ex Somerset Coast-59	1958	1,326	235	36	11½	M(A)
Gomba Progress ex Dorset Queen -74, ex Dorset-brook-72, Sprightly-69	1957	1,328	235	36	11	M(A)

JOHN GRANT (SHIPPING LINES) LTD

Ipswich

FUNNEL: None.
HULL: Grey with black boot-topping.

Name	Built	Tons	Length	Breadth	Speed	Engines
Celtic	1903	153	90	23	7	M(2)(A)

G. E. GRAY & SONS (SHIPPING) LTD
(Thos. Watson (Shipping) Ltd)

Gravesend

FUNNEL: As Watson.
HULL: Blue with black boot-topping.

Name	Built	Tons	Length	Breadth	Speed	Engines
Graybank ex Hillswick-68, Greta-64	1957	382	156	26	10	M(A)

See also Thos. Watson (Shipping) Ltd

GREATER LONDON COUNCIL

London

FUNNEL: Pale yellow with black top and Council's armorial shield in full colour.
HULL: Black with white line and red boot-topping.

Name	Built	Tons	Length	Breadth	Speed	Engines
Woolwich Ferries:						
Ernest Bevin	1963	738	186	63	8	M(F & A)
James Newman	1963	738	186	63	8	M(F & A)
John Burns	1963	738	186	63	8	M(F & A)
Sludge Carriers:						
Bexley	1966	2,175	295	50	12	M(2)(A)
Edward Cruse	1954	1,818	274	44	11	SR(2)(A)
Hounslow	1968	2,132	295	50	12	M(2)(A)
Newham	1968	2,175	295	50	12	M(2)(A)

GREENHITHE LIGHTERAGE CO LTD

Greenhithe

FUNNEL: Yellow with black top.
HULL: Green with white line and red boot-topping.

Name	Built	Tons	Length	Breadth	Speed	Engines
Ferrocrete	1927	158	104	21	7	M(3)(A)

J. H. K. GRIFFEN

Cardiff

FUNNEL: White with black top.
HULL: Black.

Name	Built	Tons	Length	Breadth	Speed	Engines
Farringay ex Empire Farringay-46	1944	461	148	28	9	M(3)(A)

HADLEY SHIPPING CO LTD

London

FUNNEL: Yellow with black top and black letters "HSC" in white diamond.
HULL: Black with red boot-topping.

Name	Built	Tons	Length	Breadth	Speed	Engines
Calandria	1970	1,477	253	39	11	M(A)
Camarina	1969	1,475	254	39	12$\frac{1}{2}$	M(A)
Corato	1969	1,476	253	39	11	M(A)
Cymbeline ex Dalewood-74	1966	5,390	370	54	13	M(A)

HALL BROS. STEAMSHIP CO LTD

Newcastle

FUNNEL: Red with black top separated by narrow white over grey over narrow white bands with replica of houseflag on grey band.
HULL: Grey with green boot-topping.

Name	Built	Tons	Length	Breadth	Speed	Engines
Bretwalda	1971	1,599	262	39	12	M(A)
Embassage	1968	1,428	253	39	12	M(A)
White Crest ex British Prince-73, White Crest-72	1971	1,587	262	39	12	M(A)

HALL DREDGING LTD
(Ready Mix Group)

London & Feltham, Middx.

FUNNEL: Orange with black "RMC" symbol or orange with narrow black top and black and orange "RMC" symbol on superstructure.
HULL: Black with orange top line.

Name	Built	Tons	Length	Breadth	Speed	Engines
Sand Dredger and Carrier:						
H. W. Wilkinson	1963	187	100	22	7½	M(A)
Harry Ford	1958	132	90	21	6½	M(2)(A)
John Gauntlett ex Gritwood-70	1963	987	200	39	9	M(A)
Joseph Hall	1963	187	100	23	7½	M(A)
Merger	1963	187	100	22	7½	M(A)
Moiler	1915	138	104	21	6½	M(A)
Sand Wader ✓	1971	3,085	316	54	13	M(A)
William Brice	1958	132	90	21	6½	M(2)(A)
Marcon R.M.C. Ltd:						
El Flamingo ✓ ex British Defender-65	1950	4,421	423	56	11	M(A)

See also Wm. Cooper & Sons Ltd

JOHN HARKER LTD

Knottingley

FUNNEL: Black with red letter "H" in red ring on white panel.
HULL: Black or black with red boot-topping.

Name	Built	Tons	Length	Breadth	Speed	Engines
Bristol Channel, Humber, Mersey and Tyne Coastal and Estuarial Tankers:						
Borrowdale H.	1972	357	166	22	9	M(A)
Deepdale H. ex Riverbeacon-67	1965	385	153	28	10	M(A)
Dovedale H. ex Riverbridge-67	1962	306	157	22	10	M(A)
Glaisdale H.	1961	303	140	22	9	M(A)
Greendale H.	1962	311	141	22	9	M(A)

John Harker Ltd (Continued)

Name	Built	Tons	Length	Breadth	Speed	Engines
Grovedale H.	1966	365	165	22	10	M(A)
Keeldale H.	1962	265	141	22	9	M(A)
Kerrydale H.	1961	255	140	22	9	M(A)
Kingsdale H.	1958	276	140	22	9	M(A)
Peakdale H.	1968	597	188	32	9	M(A)
Tynedale H.	1952	298	152	22	9	M(A)
Weasdale H.	1960	270	135	21	9	M(A)
Winsdale H.	1962	270	141	22	9	M(A)

These are representatives of the fleet, many other tank barges operate on various inland and estuaral waterways

HARRISON'S (CLYDE) LTD

Glasgow

FUNNEL: Red with black top.
HULL: Black with ted boot-topping.

Name	Built	Tons	Length	Breadth	Speed	Engines
Virgilia	1970	1,437	253	39	12	M(A)

HAY & CO (LERWICK) LTD

Lerwick

FUNNEL: Yellow with blue letter "H" on red over white over red bands.
HULL: Grey with black boot-topping.

Name	Built	Tons	Length	Breadth	Speed	Engines
Lerwick Trader ex Shetland Trader 1-72, Shetland Trader- 72, Henriette B.-64	1957	499	178	29	10	M(A)
Shetland Trader ex Tramp-72	1963	499	185	30	10½	M(A)

J. A. HAYWOOD

Fareham

FUNNEL: Red with black top.
HULL: Black with red boot-topping.

Name	Built	Tons	Length	Breadth	Speed	Engines
Sand Dredger:						
Essex Lady	1940	145	101	26	7½	DE(A)

S. HEALING & SONS LTD

Tewkesbury

FUNNEL: None.
HULL: Green with black boot-topping.

Name	Built	Tons	Length	Breadth	Speed	Engines
Deerhurst*	1933	158	101	22	7½	M(A)

* Tows dumb barges Apperley, 145/33 or Bushley, 145/34

PETER M. HERBERT
(Herb Ship Ltd)

Bude

FUNNEL: Yellow with red letter "H".
HULL: Various colours.

Name	Built	Tons	Length	Breadth	Speed	Engines
Despatch ex Atlas-37	1931	199	115	21	7	M(A)
Glenshira	1953	152	86	20	8	M(A)
Severn Stream	1951	137	90	20	7½	M(A)

J. T. HILLIER

London

FUNNEL: Blue with white letter "H".
HULL: Black with red boot-topping.

Name	Built	Tons	Length	Breadth	Speed	Engines
Isle of Harris ex Floro-65, ex Maria S.-62	1949	274	142	24	9	M(A)

M. F. HORLOCK (DREDGING) CO LTD

Oxford

FUNNEL: None.
HULL: Black.

Name	Built	Tons	Length	Breadth	Speed	Engines
Sand Dredgers and Carriers:						
Adieu	1929	109	93	19	6½	M(2)(A)

I. M. HOUSTON

London

FUNNEL: None.
HULL: Grey with black boot-topping.

Name	Built	Tons	Length	Breadth	Speed	Engines
Raybel	1920	102	87	21	7	M(A)(2)

HOVERINGHAM GRAVELS LTD

Millwall

FUNNEL: Orange-brown with black mastodon device.
HULL: Black.

Name	Built	Tons	Length	Breadth	Speed	Engines
Sand Dredgers and Carriers:						
Hoveringham I	1966	897	204	36	10	M(A)
Hoveringham III	1954	471	160	31	10	M(A)
ex Gaist-67						
Hoveringham IV	1969	1,027	236	60	10	M(A)
Hoveringham V	1969	879	208	59	10	M(A)
Hoveringham VI	1971	1,550	264	46	11	M(A)

D. HUDSON

Leigh-on-Sea

FUNNEL: Black with black letters "LS" on pale blue band.
HULL: Grey with black boot-topping.

Name	Built	Tons	Length	Breadth	Speed	Engines
Nova L	1939	234	122	22	7½	M(A)
ex Golden Bridge -74, Nova-73, Käthe Theunert-54						

JOHN HUDSON FUEL & SHIPPING LTD

Brighton

FUNNEL: Dark blue with white letter "H" on broad white band.
HULL: Black with red boot-topping.

Name	Built	Tons	Length	Breadth	Speed	Engines
Hudson Light	1965	5,628	370	54	12	M(A)
The Thornhope Shipping Co Ltd:						
New	1975	11,000dw			13½	M(A)

HULL GATES SHIPPING CO LTD
(Fred Parkes Holdings Ltd)

Grimsby

FUNNEL: Red with narrow black top and black letters "FP" on black bordered white oval.
HULL: Blue-grey with green boot-topping; or dark blue or black with white line and red boot-topping.

Name	Built	Tons	Length	Breadth	Speed	Engines
Irishgate	1965	800	201	32	12	M(A)
Northgate	1964	499	165	29	10	M(A)
Parkesgate	1972	798	200	33	12	M(A)
Simonsgate	1968	2,889	316	48	13	M(A)
ex Hansel-74						
Wellowgate	1967	300	163	30	10½	M(A)
ex Susanne Scan -74						
Coastal Tankers:						
Hullgate	1970	1,594	293	42	12½	M(A)
Humbergate	1969	1,579	278	44	12	M(A)

See also Fleetwood Tankers Ltd

IMPERIAL CHEMICAL INDUSTRIES LTD

London

FUNNEL: Blue with black top and "ICI" device in white on red disc.
HULL: Black with red or salmon boot-topping.

Name	Built	Tons	Length	Breadth	Speed	Engines
Nobel's Explosive Co Ltd:						
Lady McGowan	1952	664	182	30	10½	M(A)
Lady Roslin	1958	698	175	32	10	M(A)
Mond Division:						
Comberbach	1948	201	103	22	8	M(A)
Cuddington	1948	201	103	22	8	M(A)
James Jackson						
Grundy	1948	201	103	22	8	M(A)
Marbury	1949	231	105	23	8	M(A)
Marston	1949	231	105	23	8	M(A)

NTER ISLAND SHIPPING, LTD

Bangor, Co. Down

FUNNEL: Orange.
HULL: Black with red boot-topping.

Name	Built	Tons	Length	Breadth	Speed	Engines
Orlock ex Avondale-74, Aegir-59, Navis-56	1950	303	144	24	8	M(A)

THE ISLAND TRANSPORT CO LTD

Cowes, I.O.W.

FUNNEL: Fluorescent red with black top.
HULL: Green with red boot-topping and "THE ISLAND TRANSPORT CO LTD" in white.

Name	Built	Tons	Length	Breadth	Speed	Engines
Arreton	1916	117	98	20	7½	M(A)
Calbourne	1951	104	91	19	8	M(2)(A)
Shalfleet	1962	103	96	19	8	M(A)

SLE OF MAN STEAM PACKET CO LTD

Douglas, I.O.M.

FUNNEL: Red with black top and black rings.
HULL: Black with red boot-topping separated by white line.

Name	Built	Tons	Length	Breadth	Speed	Engines
Passenger, Car and Vehicle Ferries:						
Ben-My-Chree	1966	2,762	344	53	21	ST(2)
King Orry	1946	2,485	345	47	21	ST(2)
Manx Maid	1962	2,724	344	53	21	ST(2)
Manxman	1955	2,495	345	50	21	ST(2)

Isle of Man Steam Packet Co Ltd (Continued)

Name	Built	Tons	Length	Breadth	Speed	Engines
Mona's Isle	1951	2,491	345	47	21	ST(2)
Mona's Queen	1972	2,998	342	55	21	M(2)
Snaefell	1948	2,489	345	47	21	ST(2)
Tynwald	1947	2,487	345	47	21	ST(2)
New	1976	3,000	342	55	21	M(2)
Cargo Vessels:						
Conister ex Spaniel-73, Brentfield-59	1955	891	224	37	11½	M(A)
Peveril	1964	1,534	220	41	12	M(A)

ISLE OF SARK SHIPPING CO LTD
(Sark Shipowners Ltd)

Guernsey, C.I.

FUNNEL: Yellow with twin golden lion device on broad black band.
HULL: Black with red boot-topping.

Name	Built	Tons	Length	Breadth	Speed	Engines
Ile de Serk ex Island Commodore-69	1941	195	98	21	8½	M(2)
La Dame de Serk ex Bateau Morgat-69, Morgat-64	1953	152	100	23	8½	M(2)

ISLES OF SCILLY STEAMSHIP CO LTD

St. Mary's, Isles of Scilly

FUNNEL: Yellow.
HULL: White with red boot-topping.

Name	Built	Tons	Length	Breadth	Speed	Engines
Scillonian	1956	921	210	33	15½	M(2)

MONA'S QUEEN, Isle of Man Steam Packet Co Ltd *J. Clarkson*

JEPPESON HEATON LTD

London

FUNNEL: Yellow with houseflag (Divided vertically, red white red with blue letter "J" on white).
HULL: White with green boot-topping.

Name	Built	Tons	Length	Breadth	Speed	Engines
Con Zelo	1957	399	165	26	10	M(A)

JERSEY CAR FERRIES LTD
(Lisarg Developments Ltd)

Jersey, C.I.

FUNNEL: Yellow with yellow letters "JCF" on blue panel.
HULL: Yellow with red boot-topping and "JERSEY CAR FERRIES" in white.

Name	Built	Tons	Length	Breadth	Speed	Engines
Jersey Queen ex Commodore Queen-73, Hein Muck-61, Rochester Queen-56	1944	309	160	25	10	M(2)

JOHN KELLY LTD

Belfast

FUNNEL: Black with red over white over blue bands with a small black letter "K" on the white band.
HULL: Dark grey with red boot-topping.

Name	Built	Tons	Length	Breadth	Speed	Engines
Ballylesson	1959	1,280	250	34	11	M(A)
Ballyloran	1958	1,092	220	34	11	M(A)
Ballymore ex Beeding-70	1950	1,277	244	35	11	M(A)
Ballyrobert ex Ardingley-71	1951	1,473	253	37	10½	M(A)
Ballyrory	1963	1,575	256	39	11½	M(A)
Ballyrush	1962	1,575	256	39	11	M(A)

John Kelly Ltd (Continued)

Name	Built	Tons	Length	Breadth	Speed	Engines
Ballywater ex Steyning-71	1955	1,572	242	38	10¾	M(A)

KENDALL BROS. (PORTSMOUTH) LTD

Portsmouth

FUNNEL: Black.
HULL: Dark green with black boot-topping.

Name	Built	Tons	Length	Breadth	Speed	Engines
Sand Dredgers and Carriers: **KB** ex Arklow-73, Eisbar-70, Herta II-63, Arctic-58, Banka-55	1948	299	136	24	8½	M(A)

F. A. G. & J. KENNEDY

Rochester

FUNNEL: Black.
HULL: Black with red boot-topping.

Name	Built	Tons	Length	Breadth	Speed	Engines
Gyrinus ex Festivity-74	1963	199	110	25	8	M(A)

KLONDYKE SHIPPING CO LTD
(May & Hassell Group)
Hull

FUNNEL: Grey with houseflag (Red bordered yellow swallowtail with black letter "K").
HULL: Grey or black with red boot-topping.

Name	Built	Tons	Length	Breadth	Speed	Engines
Fendyke	1971	696	208	33	$12\frac{1}{4}$	M(A)
Framptondyke	1964	1,599	281	42	12	M(A)
Kirtondyke	1957	959	215	35	12	M(A)
Somersbydyke	1967	1,598	302	44	$11\frac{1}{2}$	M(A)
Westondyke	1971	696	208	33	12	M(A)
New	1974		280	43	$13\frac{1}{2}$	M(A)
May & Hassel Ltd, Bristol:						
New	1974	2,450dw				M(A)

J. P. KNIGHT (LONDON) LTD
London

FUNNEL: Black with two silver bands and silver letter "K".
HULL: Black.

Name	Built	Tons	Length	Breadth	Speed	Engines
Effluent Tankers:						
Kingsabbey	1928	351	158	24	7	M(A)
ex Fealtie-66						
Kingsclere	1956	303	139	22	8	M(A)/VS
ex Shell Steelmaker-69						
Kingsthorpe	1956	303	140	22	8	M(A)/VS
ex B.P. Manufacturer-69						

See also Tugs

K. W. M. LINE LTD

Ipswich

FUNNEL: Blue with blue letters "KWM" on white band.
HULL: Dark grey with black boot-topping.

Name	Built	Tons	Length	Breadth	Speed	Engines
Bristol Trader ex Nordsee- Karin-72, Milos- 65	1951	425	164	25	9	M(A)

I. P. LANGFORD (SHIPPING) LTD

Sharpness

FUNNEL: Red with black top and large white letter "L".
HULL: Grey with red boot-topping.

Name	Built	Tons	Length	Breadth	Speed	Engines
Effluent Tankers:						
Fulham ex Empire Fulham-74	1944	222	100	23	8	M(A)
Kyles	1872*	121	82	18	7	M(A)

* *Rebuilt 1945*

R. LAPTHORN & CO LTD

Rochester

FUNNEL: Red with black band with yellow star superimposed.
HULL: Black with grey topsides, grey with black boot-topping or black with red boot-topping.

Name	Built	Tons	Length	Breadth	Speed	Engines
Hoocrest ex Ida D.-70	1955	490	169	27	10	M(A)
Hoofort ex Ramsey-74	1965	446	159	29	11	M(A)
Hoopride ex Berend N-74, Martenshoeck- 74	1961	460	163	26	10	M(A)
Hootact ex Contact-70, Gesina-52	1950	263	135	23	8½	M(A)

R. Lapthorn & Co Ltd (Continued)

Name	Built	Tons	Length	Breadth	Speed	Engines
City of London Tankers Ltd, London:						
Hootern ex Dolphin City-74, Dolphin G.-73, Martinistad-71	1957	490	174	28	9½	M(A)
Eddystone Shipping Co Ltd, Hoo Kent:						
Edward Stone	1965	196	109	22	7	M(A)
Springwell Shipping Co Ltd, Hull:						
Hoofinch	1964	332	145	26	9½	M(A)

LE BLOND SHIPPING CO

South Shields

FUNNEL: White with red letters "LB" between narrow red bands.
HULL: Blue with red boot-topping.

Name	Built	Tons	Length	Breadth	Speed	Engines
Solway Firth* ex G. R. Velie-74 ex Carnissesingel 66	1958	506	178	29	9½	M(A)
GRANVILLE *EX BATTERSEA*	1951	1.777	271	40	11	M/A

* Registered Cork

B. P. LEONARD

London

FUNNEL: White with red top and red and white Maltese cross.
HULL:

Name	Built	Tons	Length	Breadth	Speed	Engines
Vehicle Ferry:						
Channelbridge I ex Malta Cross-72	1970	407	223	43	10	M(A)

LINCOLN & HULL MARINE CONTRACTORS LTD

Hull

FUNNEL: None.
HULL: Black.

Name	Built	Tons	Length	Breadth	Speed	Engines
Besthorpe	1964	218	137	21	7	M(A)
Collingham	1973	356	146	28	8	M(A)
Girton	1964	218	137	21	7	M(A)
Laneham	1965	218	137	21	7	M(A)
Linklight*	1949	143	93	21	6	M(2)(A)
Marnham	1968	253	144	23	7	M(A)
Normanton	1967	218	137	21	7	M(A)
Swanmore*	1930	149	120	21	6	M(A)

* Crane barge fitted with 22 RB Excavator

W. N. LINDSAY (SHIPOWNERS) LTD

Leith

FUNNEL: Red with black top separated by blue band.
HULL: Black with red boot-topping.

Name	Built	Tons	Length	Breadth	Speed	Engines
Rosewell* ex Hotwells-70	1950	499	163	27	9	M(A)
W. N. Lindsay Ltd:						
Roselyne ex Pamela C.-73, Plancius-72	1955	498	189	28	9	M(A)
Rosemarkie ex Marinex III- 73, Jovista-70, Petro Minor-68, Jovista-66, Thuban-64	1947	554	201	30	10	M(A)

* Voe Shipping Ltd., Lerwick

LLANELLI PLANT HIRE CO LTD

Llanelli

FUNNEL: Yellow with red letters.
HULL: Grey with black boot-topping.

Name	Built	Tons	Length	Breadth	Speed	Engines
Sand Dredger and Carrier:						
Rhone	1966	276	152	25	9½	M(A)

LONDON & ROCHESTER TRADING CO LTD

Rochester

FUNNEL: Black with white crescent on broad red band between narrow white bands.
HULL: Red brown with white or blue topline and red boot-topping.

Name	Built	Tons	Length	Breadth	Speed	Engines
Ambience	1969	392	146	26	9	M(A)
Andescol	1961	191	100	22	8	M(A)
Bastion	1958	172	96	22	7	M(A)
Bencol	1964	204	105	23	9	M(A)
Blatence	1969	392	146	26	9	M(A)
Cadence	1969	392	146	26	9	M(A)
Caption	1963	189	105	24	8¼	M(A)
Cecil Gilders	1957	137	91	21	8	M(2)(A)
Crescence	1965	999	221	35	12	M(A)
Dangeld*	1969	694	247	41	13¼	M(A)
Diction	1963	189	105	24	8¼	M(A)
Dominence	1970	425	157	29	9	M(A)
Elation	1963	212	99	22	9	M(A)
Eloquence	1969	392	146	26	9	M(A)
Eminence	1969	999	220	39	11	M(A)
Faience	1969	424	157	29	10	M(A)
Fallow Deer†	1972	497	252	43	13¾	M(A)
Function	1963	212	100	22	9	M(A)
Gardience	1969	424	157	29	10	M(A)
Gillation	1964	195	102	22	8¼	M(A)
Halcience	1970	424	157	29	10	M(A)
Horation	1964	205	106	23	9	M(A)
Ignition	1967	199	105	23	8½	M(A)
Josh Francis	1954	137	85	20	6½	M(2)(A)
Jubilation	1967	199	106	23	8½	M(A)
Kiption	1968	198	106	23	8½	M(A)

* *White Hull*

† *On charter to European Unit Routes and operating in their colours*

Top: FALLOW DEER, London & Rochester Trading Co Ltd *F. R. Sherlock*

GOOSANDER, Ministry of Defence (Navy) *M.O.D. (Navy)*

London & Rochester Trading Co Ltd (Continued)

Name	Built	Tons	Length	Breadth	Speed	Engines
Libation	1969	198	100	22	8	M(A)
Loach	1968	191	104	22	6¾	M(2)(A)
Lobe	1968	191	104	22	6½	M(2)(A)
Locator	1970	194	104	22	6½	M(2)(A)
Lodella	1971	196	104	22	6½	M(2)(A)
Maguda	1959	170	90	22	8	M(A)
Maloney	1952	124	85	20	7	M(2)(A)
Nicola Dawn	1955	137	86	21	7	M(2)(A)
Pepita	1955	137	86	21	7	M(2)(A)
Pertinence	1958	868	206	32	10½	M(A)
Quiescence	1959	868	206	32	10½	M(A)
Resilience**	1969	988	218	37	12¾	M(A)
Resurgence ex De Paarse Tulp-74, Petro Topaz-73, Petro Queen-71	1967	1,198	244	37	10	M(A)
Rogul	1965	172	96	22	8	M(A)
Rohoy	1966	172	96	22	8	M(A)
Roina	1966	172	96	22	8	M(A)
Sentence	1974	999	222	38	11¾	M(A)
Spartan	1898	106	85	21	6½	M(2)(A)
Stargate ex Wilfred-53	1926	106	88	21	6	M(2)(A)
New	1974	660dw				M(A)
New	1974	660dw				M(A)
B. T. Cuckow *Rochester:*						
Silver	1952	120	85	20	7	M(2)(A)

M. Lynch & Son, Rochester: (La Mouette Shipping Corp):

Name	Built	Tons	Length	Breadth	Speed	Engines
Jo‡ ex Kars-70, Superior Trader- 68, Kars-67	1955	420	149	24	10	M(A)

R. W. Witts, Minster, Isle of Sheppey:

Name	Built	Tons	Length	Breadth	Speed	Engines
Gold	1951	120	85	20	7	M(2)(A)
Maralie ex Hollandie-70, Holland-62	1951	310	148	25	8½	M(A)

* White Hull

† On charter to European Unit Routes and operating in their colours

** Starch Tanker

‡ Panamanian flag

See also Tugs

COMBEN LONGSTAFF & CO LTD
(Amey Roadstone Corp Ltd)

London

FUNNEL: Black with red letters "CL" on white diamond on broad red band.
HULL: Black with red boot-topping.

Name	Built	Tons	Length	Breadth	Speed	Engines
Caernarvonbrook	1964	1,594	265	39	12	M(A)
Chesterbrook	1963	1,594	265	39	12	M(A)
Clarebrook	1964	1,594	265	39	12	M(A)
Cornishbrook	1961	1,595	260	39	12	M(A)
Autovan Shipping Co *(Ugland Management Co A/S colours):*						
Vehicle Carrier:						
Autostrada	1971	610	303	48	14½	M(A)
M. K. Bustard:						
George Armfield ex Winchester- brook-74	1960	1,102	217	34	11½	M(A)
County Ships Ltd:						
Corkbrook	1964	1,594	265	39	12	M(A)
Solentbrook	1972	1,597	283	42	12¾	M(A)
Somersetbrook	1971	1,596	283	42	12	M(A)
Stirlingbrook	1970	1,597	283	42	12	M(A)
Surreybrook	1971	1,596	283	42	12	M(A)
Sussexbrook	1970	1,596	283	42	12	M(A)

See also ARC Marine Ltd and Eskgarth Shipping Co Ltd

LUNDY ISLAND CO LTD
(National Trust Ltd)

London

FUNNEL: Yellow with black top.
HULL: Red.

Name	Built	Tons	Length	Breadth	Speed	Engines
Polar Bear ex Agdleq-71	1960	222	113	22	9	M(A)

Lundy Island Service

MacANDREWS & CO LTD
(United Baltic Corp Ltd)

London

FUNNEL: Yellow.
HULL: White with green boot-topping.

Name	Built	Tons	Length	Breadth	Speed	Engines
Cervantes	1968	1,593	301	44	16½	M(A)
Churruca	1968	1,577	301	44	16½	M(A)
Palacio	1961	1,096	248	42	16	M(A)
Palomares	1963	1,196	245	42	16	M(A)

See also United Baltic Corporation Ltd

P. MacCALLUM & SONS LTD

Greenock

FUNNEL: Red with black top and black rings.
HULL: Grey with red boot-topping.

Name	Built	Tons	Length	Breadth	Speed	Engines
Ardgarvel	1965	1,121	223	35	11	M(A)

MALDON SHIPPING CO LTD

Maldon

FUNNEL: Green with yellow letter "B" between narrow yellow bands.
HULL: Green with white topline and black boot-toppings.

Name	Built	Tons	Length	Breadth	Speed	Engines
Sand Dredgers and Carriers:						
Bill Brush ex Maureen Brush-69, C. 621-61	1944	192	106	23	7½	M(A)

MANCHE SHIPPING CO LTD

Jersey, C.I.

FUNNEL: Yellow with dark blue band.
HULL: Grey with black boot-topping.

Name	Built	Tons	Length	Breadth	Speed	Engines
Sorel ex Lady Sandra-68	1958	356	149	24	10	M(A)

MARDORF, PEACH & CO LTD

London

FUNNEL: Yellow "Sunblest" motif on white disc on red funnel with black top separated by narrow white over narrow black bands.
HULL: Light grey with blue or red boot-topping.

Name	Built	Tons	Length	Breadth	Speed	Engines
Camilla Weston ex Crouch-71	1966	500	184	29	10½	M(A)
Catrina Weston	1971	425	147	29	9	M(A)
Edward Brough	1974	425	157	29	10	M(A)
Gretchen Weston ex Deben-71	1966	500	183	29	10½	M(A)
Guy Chipperfield	1974	425	157	29	10	M(A)
Jana Weston	1971	500	183	33	10	M(A)
Mary Weston	1973	496				M(A)
Sophia Weston	1972	425	157	29	10	M(A)

Weston Shipping (Managers). (Funnel: Red with black top separated by white over green bands. Hull: Grey with black boot-topping.)

Name	Built	Tons	Length	Breadth	Speed	Engines
Frederick Hughes	1936	311	135	25	8½	M(A)

MARINE DISPOSALS (HOLDINGS) LTD

Preesall, Nr. Blackpool

FUNNEL: Black with red letters "MDH" on white disc on pale blue band.
HULL: Black.

Name	Built	Tons	Length	Breadth	Speed	Engines
Effluent Tanker:						

Name	Built	Tons	Length	Breadth	Speed	Engines
Glamardis ex Wandale H.- 68	1952	262	136	22	8½	M(A)

MARINEX GRAVELS LTD

Cliffe

FUNNEL: Blue with Company symbol in white.
HULL: Blue with red boot-topping.

Name	Built	Tons	Length	Breadth	Speed	Engines
Sand Dredgers and Carriers:						
Marinex V	1971	2,825	289	53	11½	M(A)
Marinex VI	1973	2,206	276	49	12	M(A)

MARPRO LTD

Surbiton

FUNNEL:
HULL: Blue-grey with green boot-topping.

Name	Built	Tons	Length	Breadth	Speed	Engines
Mariyos I ex Foxtongate-74	1963	718	197	30	10	M(A)

E. F. McGUINNESS

Wateringbury, Essex

FUNNEL: White with houseflag and blue top (Houseflag; blue with white letter "M").
HULL: Black with green boot-topping.

Name	Built	Tons	Length	Breadth	Speed	Engines
Manta	1951	366	149	24	10	M(A)

MERSEYSIDE PASSENGER TRANSPORT EXECUTIVE
(Wirral Division (Ferries))

Liverpool

FUNNEL: Cream with blue top or *white with blue band.
HULL: Black with red line and red boot-topping or *dark blue with red boot-topping.

Name	Built	Tons	Length	Breadth	Speed	Engines
Mersey Ferries:						
Egremont	1952	566	146	38	13	M(2)
Mountwood	1960	464	152	41	12½	M(2)
Overchurch	1962	468	153	41	12½	M(2)
Royal Daffodil	1958	609	160	49	12	M(2)
ex Royal Daffodil II-68						
Royal Iris*	1951	1,234	159	50	13	DE(2)
Woodchurch	1960	464	152	41	12½	M(2)

Royal Iris is used for dining and cruising and does not operate normal ferry services

METCALF MOTOR COASTERS LTD
(Brooker McConnell)

London

FUNNEL: Green with or without black top and large white letter "M".
HULL: Black with red or green boot-topping.

Name	Built	Tons	Length	Breadth	Speed	Engines
Ann M.	1961	1,203	230	37	11½	M(A)
Christopher M.	1956	1,035	218	34	11	M(A)
Eileen M.	1966	861	200	35	11½	M(A)
Marian M.	1955	694	195	32	11	M(A)
Mary M	1958	1,097	222	35	10½	M(A)
ex Yewforest-74						
Melissa M.	1956	1,089	230	34	12	M(A)
Michael M.	1955	691	195	31	11	M(A)
Nellie M.	1972	783	203	34	12	M(A)
Coastal Tankers:						
Frank M.	1965	1,307	232	37	11	M(A)
John M.	1963	1,308	230	37	11	M(A)
Nicholas M.	1966	1,308	232	37	11	M(A)

Metcalf Motor Coasters Ltd. (Continued)

Name	Built	Tons	Length	Breadth	Speed	Engines
C. Crawley Ltd, Gravesend: Fresh Water Tanker:						
Aquajet ex E. B. Spearing -74, British Maiden-73	1924	102	90	19	7	M(A)
Aquatic ex Bannister-73, Skelmunjer-56, Scot-47, Empire Lundy-46	1944	227	143	21	9	M(A)

See also S. W. Coe & Co Ltd

MIDDLE MERSEY EFFLUENT TREATMENT UNIT

Manchester

FUNNEL: Yellow with black top and armorial shield.
HULL: Black with red boot-topping.

Name	Built	Tons	Length	Breadth	Speed	Engines
Sludge Carrier:						
Consortium I	1972	2,548	298	47	13	M(2)(A)
Gilbert J. Fowler	1971	2,548	298	47	12¾	M(2)(A)
Mancunian	1946	1,390	263	38	12	M(2)(A)
Percy Dawson	1968	1,525	258	41	12¾	M(2)(A)
Salford City	1928	1,179	241	38	12	SR(2)(A)

MILTON SHIPPING CO LTD
(Denholm Maclay Co Ltd)

Glasgow

FUNNEL: Yellow with black top separated by narrow white band.
HULL: Black with red boot-topping.

Name	Built	Tons	Length	Breadth	Speed	Engines
Mingary	1972	1,599	287	39	12	M(A)
Moidart	1972	1,599	287	39	12	M(A)

MINISTRY OF DEFENCE (NAVY)
(Royal Maritime Auxiliary Service)

London

FUNNEL: Grey with black top.
HULL: Black.

Name	Built	Tons	Length	Breadth	Speed	Engines
Mooring, Boom and Salvage Vessels:						
Barfoot	1942	626	174*	32	9	SR
Dispenser	1943	775	179*	35	9	SR
Felsted	1969	112	80	21	11	M(A)
Goosander	1973	923	197	40	10	M
Kingarth ex Sledway	1944	775	179*	35	9	M
Kinloss	1945	775	179*	35	9	M
Layburn	1960		193*	35	10	SR
Mandarin	1963	765	183*	37	10	M
Miner 3	1939		110	27	10	M(2)
Pochard	1973	923	197	40	10	M
Scarab	1970	279	112	30	11½	M(A)
Uplifter	1943	775	179*	35	10	M
Cable Ships:						
Bullfinch	1940	1,524	252	37	12	SR
St. Margarets	1943	1,524	252	37	12	SR
Experimental Vessel:						
Whitehead (A. 364)	1970	2,500	319	48	15½	M(A)

* *Add approximately 10 ft to include horns*

MINISTRY OF DEFENCE (NAVY)
(Royal Fleet Auxiliary)

London

FUNNEL: Grey with black top.
HULL: Grey with black boot-topping.

Name	Built	Tons	Length	Breadth	Speed	Engines
Coastal Tanker:						
Eddyfirth (A. 261)	1953	2,300	286	44	12	SR(A)
Coastal Store Carrier:						

Name	Built	Tons	Length	Breadth	Speed	Engines
Robert Middleton (A. 241)	1938	1,085	220	35	10½	M(A)

MINISTRY OF DEFENCE (NAVY)
(Director of Marine Services)

FUNNEL : Yellow with black top with white bordered or plain red or blue bands.

HULL : Black with blue, red or white line and red boot-topping.

Name	Built	Tons	Length	Breadth	Speed	Engines
Ammunition Carriers:						
Kinterbury	1943	889	200	34	11	SR(A)
Maxim*	1944	392	134	25	9	SR(A)
Throsk	1943	901	200	34	11	SR(A)
Torpedo Recovery Vessels:						
Torrent	1971	660	151	28	12	M
Torrid	1971	660	151	28	12	M
Tank Cleaning Vessels:						
Bern ex HMS Bern-56	1942	478	164	28	10	SR
Caldy ex HMS Caldy-51	1943	460	164	27	10	SR
Graemsay ex HMS Graemsay-56	1942	475	164	28	10	SR
Lundy ex HMS Lundy-56	1942	475	164	28	10	SR
Skomer ex HMS Skomer-56	1943	460	164	27	10	SR
Switha ex HMS Switha-50	1942	475	164	28	10	SR

* Laid up at Pembroke Dock
See also Harbour Works & Dredging Craft and Tugs

H. R. MITCHELL & SONS LTD

Woolwich

FUNNEL: Yellow with or without black top.
HULL: Black with red boot-topping or colours of previous owner.

Name	Built	Tons	Length	Breadth	Speed	Engines
Harry Mitchell ex Zwaantiena-74	1953	385	154	25	9	M(A)
John Mitchell ex Speranza-72	1958	384	157	26	9	M(A)
Katharine Mitchell	1930	177	114	22	8½	M(2)(A)
May Mitchell ex Corbiere-71, Lerwick-68, Rema-63	1950	372	157	25	9½	M(A)
Patricia Mitchell ex Patricia-68, Britannia-56, Polonia-52, Kragnaes-48, Cranz-47	1938	226	128	22	11	M(A)

MOBIL SHIPPING CO LTD

London

FUNNEL: Black with "MOBIL" in blue and red on white panel.
HULL: Grey with black boot-topping.

Name	Built	Tons	Length	Breadth	Speed	Engines
Coastal Oil/Chemical Tanker:						
Mobil Lubchem	1973	2,080	306	46	12¾	M(A)

J. R. L. MOORE

London

FUNNEL: As Shell-Mex & B.P. Ltd (on charter).
HULL: Black.

Name	Built	Tons	Length	Breadth	Speed	Engines
Thames Tanker:						
St. Leonards	1964	215	117	27	9½	M(A)

NORLINE LTD

Maldon

FUNNEL: Yellow with yellow "NL" monogram on red shield.
HULL: Blue with red boot-topping.

Name	Built	Tons	Length	Breadth	Speed	Engines
Samnor ex Lady Sybilla-73, Vitesse-59	1952	325	149	24	10	M(A)

NORMANDIE DREDGING AND SHIPPING CO LTD
(J. N. Callaghan)

Southampton

FUNNEL: Red with houseflag (White swallowtail with black letter "N").
HULL: Black with red boot-topping.

Name	Built	Tons	Length	Breadth	Speed	Engines
Sand Dredgers and Carriers						
Seastone ex James No. 46-61, P.L.A. Hopper No. 7, Thames Conservancy Hopper-No. 7	1907	861	204	32	9	M(A)
Solent Lee ex Oarsman-73	1959	778	204	31	10	M(A)
Lee Shipping Ltd:						
Humber Lee ex Clonlee-73, Calcium-65	1959	643	183	32	10½	M(A)

NORFOLK LINE LTD

Gt. Yarmouth

FUNNEL: Cream with Company symbol in black, blue, white and red and black top.
HULL:

Name	Built	Tons	Length	Breadth	Speed	Engines
Vehicle Ferry:						
Duke of Norfolk	1972	948	258	47	13½	M(A)

NORTH OF SCOTLAND, ORKNEY & SHETLAND SHIPPING CO LTD
(P & O Group)

Aberdeen

FUNNEL: Yellow.
HULL: Black with red boot-topping separated by white line.

Name	Built	Tons	Length	Breadth	Speed	Engines
Earl of Zetland	1939	548	166	29	12	M
St. Clair	1960	2,864	296	50	14	M
St. Clement	1946	815	188	31	11½	M(A)
St. Magnus	1955	871	242	36	12½	M(A)
ex City of Dublin-66						
St. Ola	1974	1,150	230	48	15	M(2)
St. Ola II	1951	750	178	33	11	M(A)
ex St. Ola-74						
St. Rognvald	1955	941	244	39	13	M(2)(A)
New	1974	750dw				M

See also Belfast Steamship Co Ltd, General Steam Navigation (Trading) Ltd, North Sea Ferries Ltd and Tyne-Tees Steam Shipping Co Ltd

NORTH SEA FERRIES LTD

(P & O Group)

Hull

FUNNEL: Orange.
HULL: Black with orange line and red boot-topping.

Name	Built	Tons	Length	Breadth	Speed	Engines
Car and Vehicle Ferries:						
Norland	1973	12,988	502	83	19	M(2)
Norwave	1965	3,540	357	62	15	M(2)
Norwind*	1966	3,692	357	62	15	M(2)

* Owned by Nordzee Veerdiensten B.V. Rotterdam (Netherlands flag)

See also Belfast Steamship Co Ltd, General Steam Navigation (Trading) Ltd, North of Scotland Orkney & Shetland Shipping Co Ltd and Tyne-Tees Steam Shipping Co Ltd

NORTHERN SHIPPING & TRADING CO (HELMSDALE) LTD

(J. C. Simpson)

Aberdeen

FUNNEL: Black with silver over red over silver bands.
HULL: Black with green boot-topping.

Name	Built	Tons	Length	Breadth	Speed	Engines
Helmsdale	1956	402	153	26	10	M(A)

Top: ST. CLAIR, North of Scotland, Orkney & Shetland Shipping Co Ltd *J. Clarkson*

WEGRO, Osborne Shipping Co Ltd *Osborne Shpg. Co*

NORTHWOOD (FAREHAM) LTD

Portsmouth

FUNNEL: Black with two white bands.
HULL: Grey with red boot-topping.

Name	Built	Tons	Length	Breadth	Speed	Engines
Sand Dredger and Carrier:						
Steel Welder ex Shell Welder-74	1955	500	171	30	8½	M(A)

FRED OLSEN LINES LTD

London

FUNNEL: Yellow with replica of houseflag (White swallowtail with diagonal blue stripe from top of hoist and blue disc in top of fly).
HULL: Grey with green boot-topping.

Name	Built	Tons	Length	Breadth	Speed	Engines
Blenheim	1970	9,248	490	66	22½	M(2)(A)

British flag subsidiary company of Fred Olsen, Bergen, Norway

ONABI SHIPPING CO

Hamilton, Bermuda

FUNNEL: Blue/green with black lettering "MAP" (Chartered to MAP Tankers Inc. New Milton).
HULL: Blue with green boot-topping.

Name	Built	Tons	Length	Breadth	Speed	Engines
Oil/Chemical Tankers:						
Odabo	1972	521	216	32	11	M(A)
Onabi	1968	565	210	32	11½	M(A)
Bobodi Shipping Ltd:						
Bobodi	1968	698	228	39	12	M(A)

ORKNEY ISLANDS SHIPPING CO LTD

Kirkwall

FUNNEL: Red with Company symbol in white between narrow white bands·
HULL: Black with red boot-topping.

Name	Built	Tons	Length	Breadth	Speed	Engines
Islander	1969	250	132	32	11	M(2)(A)
Secretary of State for Scotland:						
Orcadia	1962	869	164	37	12	M(A)

OSBORNE SHIPPING CO LTD

Brighton

FUNNEL: Blue with white "CRR" monogram.
HULL: Grey with black boot-topping.

Name	Built	Tons	Length	Breadth	Speed	Engines
Wegro	1955	485	169	28	$9\frac{1}{2}$	M(A)

OVALPORT LTD

London

FUNNEL: Black.
HULL: Black.

Name	Built	Tons	Length	Breadth	Speed	Engines
Coastal and Estuaral Tanker:						
Patmaldon I ex Kirkdale H-74	1957	276	140	22	9	M(A)

K. A. PACK & G. J. WARNES

Ipswich

FUNNEL:
HULL:

Name	Built	Tons	Length	Breadth	Speed	Engines
Meppel	1939	249	128	23	9	M(A)
Rito	1950	400	155	26	9	M(A)
ex Triton-73						

T. J. PALMER & SONS

Gravesend

FUNNEL: Blue with or without narrow black top and large white letter "F
HULL: Dark green with red boot-topping.

Name	Built	Tons	Length	Breadth	Speed	Engines
Brandram	1915	158	104	21	7	M(A)
ex Cawarstone						
Gazelle	1904	166	90	23	8	M(2)(A
ex Goldrune-51, Runic-49						
Glas Island	1935	211	104	24	7	M(2)(A
ex Lady Stella-55						
Lafford	1957	138	90	21	8	M(2)(A
Subro Viking	1962	296	150	26	10½	M(A)
ex Thuroklint-73						
Queenford	1959	200	118	25	9	M(A)
ex Rye Trader-72, Polarlight-69, Queensgate-65						

PANOCEAN LLOYD GmbH

(Panocean Shipping & Terminals Ltd London & Hamburger Lloyd GmbH Hamburg)

Hamburg

FUNNEL: Yellow with four narrow black bands.
HULL: Grey with red boot-topping.

Name	Built	Tons	Length	Breadth	Speed	Engines
Rhine Chemical Tankers:						
Alchimist London	1973	969	274	31	11	M(A)
Alchimist Liverpool	1973	999	274	31	11	M(A)

Both vessels operate under the British flag

PELHAM DALE PARTNERS LTD

Rye

FUNNEL: Black.
HULL: Grey with black-topping.

Name	Built	Tons	Length	Breadth	Speed	Engines
Waterdale ex Walter Richter-72	1957	423	174	29	9	M(A)

J. R. PIPER LTD

Greenwich

FUNNEL: None.
HULL: Black with red boot-topping.

Name	Built	Tons	Length	Breadth	Speed	Engines
Beverley Brook	1941	245	130	25	8	M(A)

A. J. PRATT

Gillingham

FUNNEL: None.
HULL: Grey or Brown with black or red boot-topping.

Name	Built	Tons	Length	Breadth	Speed	Engines
Milligan	1952	124	85	20	7	M(2)(A)
A. J. Pratt &						
Annette Pratt:						
Seaclose	1954	110	90	20	8	M(2)(A)

PRINCE LINE LTD
(Furness Withy Group)

London

FUNNEL: Black with red over black over broad red bands with white Prince of Wales feathers.
HULL: Pale grey with red boot-topping.

Name	Built	Tons	Length	Breadth	Speed	Engines
Chiltern Prince	1970	1,499	285	47	13½	M(A)
Cotswold Prince	1970	1,459	285	47	13½	M(A)
Malvern Prince	1970	1,459	285	47	13½	M(A)
Cheviot Prince	1970	1,459	285	47	13½	M(A)
ex Mendip						
Prince-74						
Sailor Prince*	1971	1,599	282	45	16	M(A)
ex Pennine						
Prince-72						

* *Owned by Pacific Maritime Services Ltd*

See also Shaw Savill & Albion Co Ltd

J. J. PRIOR (TRANSPORT) LTD

London

FUNNEL: Red with black top.
HULL: Black.

Name	Built	Tons	Length	Breadth	Speed	Engines
Sand Carriers:						

J. J. Prior (Transport) Ltd (Continued)

Name	Built	Tons	Length	Breadth	Speed	Engines
A.H.P. ✓ ex Admiralty X-Lighter	1917	175	105	21	7	M(A)
Bert Prior	1963	175	96	22	9	M(A)
Colin P. ex Leah P.-73, Betty Hudson-64 Admiralty X-Lighter	1915	172	105	21	7	M(A)
Colne Trader ex Walcrag-62, Springcrag-54, Empire Crag-46	1941	329	136	25	9	M(A)
James P. ✓	1963	191	103	22	8	M(A)
Leonard P. ex James M.-64, Admiralty X-Lighter	1915	174	106	21	7	M(A)
Peter P.	1915	186	105	21	6½	M(A)
Sidney P. ex Sway-64, Admiralty X-Lighter	1915	162	105	21	7	M(A)

RAMSEY STEAMSHIP CO LTD

Ramsey, I.O.M.

FUNNEL : Black with white Maltese cross on red bands.
HULL : Grey with red boot-topping.

Name	Built	Tons	Length	Breadth	Speed	Engines
Ben Varrey	1963	440	170	28	10¾	M(A)
Ben Veen ex Plover-71	1965	486	161	29	12	M(A)
Ben Veg	1965	346	144	26	8½	M(A)
Ben Vooar ex Mudo-59	1950	427	160	27	8½	M(A)

REA LTD

Liverpool

FUNNEL: In colours of Bulk Cargo Handling Services Ltd.
HULL: Black with red boot-topping.

Name	Built	Tons	Length	Breadth	Speed	Engines
Pickerel ex Petro-72	1939	444	162	32	8½	M(A)

REXERTER LTD

London

FUNNEL: None.
HULL: White with blue quarter.

Name	Built	Tons	Length	Breadth	Speed	Engines
Thames Excursions and Restaurant Vessels:						
Father Thames	1971	453	155	25	8	M(2)(A)

J. J. RILEY (UK) LTD

Longfield, Kent

FUNNEL:
HULL:

Name	Built	Tons	Length	Breadth	Speed	Engines
Sand Dredger and Carrier:						
Stone Marshall ex Needwood-72	1966/7	1,555	278	46	10	M(A)

RISDON BEAZLEY, MARINE LTD
(Smit Tak Group)

Southampton

FUNNEL: Red with black grapnel on white panel with or without black top.
HULL: Black with red boot-topping.

Name	Built	Tons	Length	Breadth	Speed	Engines
Salvage Craft:						
Droxford	1958	1,302	226	37	11½	SR
Lifeline	1944	752	179	36	9¾	M
Queen Mother	1944	184	102	23	9	M
Topmast 16	1943	434	192	30	5	M(2)(A)
ex Segundo-64						
Topmast 18	1942	497	195	31	7½	M(2)(A)
ex Rampino-64						
Topmast 20	1942	485	204	31	7½	M(2)(A)
Twyford	1952	1,104	221	36	12	SR

Also the floating crane Magnus II—400 ton lift

J. R. RIX & SONS LTD

Hull

FUNNEL: Red with black top and white "JR" monogram on red diamond on broad blue band. (Whitehaven Shipping Co vessels have blue bordered red diamond).
HULL: Green with white topline and red boot-topping.

Name	Built	Tons	Length	Breadth	Speed	Engines
Fylrix	1962	637	189	28	10½	M(A)
Salrix	1965	763	214	32	12	M(A)
ex Owenro-73						
Timrix	1965	499	194	33	11	M(A)
ex Majo-72						
Whitehaven Shipping Co Ltd:						
Kenrix	1960	635	204	28	10½	M(A)
Lesrix	1957	726	185	33	10½	M(A)
ex Whitehaven-63						
Highseas Ltd:						
Bobrix	1957	584	180	29	10	M(A)

A. W. ROBERTS

Rochester

FUNNEL: Yellow with black top.
HULL: Grey with black boot-topping.

Name	Built	Tons	Length	Breadth	Speed	Engines
Vectis Isle ex Badzo-59	1939	213	123	21	8¾	M(A)

WILLIAM ROBERTSON, SHIPOWNERS, LTD
(Stephenson Clarke Ltd)

Glasgow

FUNNEL: Black.
HULL: Black with red boot-topping.

Name	Built	Tons	Length	Breadth	Speed	Engines
Amber	1956	1,596	268	39	12½	M(A)
Amethyst	1958	1,548	258	40	12	M(A)
Brilliant	1958	1,143	224	34	11	M(A)
Cairngorm	1973	1,598	316	46	14½	M(A)
Cameo ex Gem-60	1952	1,597	275	40	10½	M(A)
Emerald	1952	1,454	241	38	10½	M(A)
Gem	1969	1,599	304	44	12	M(A)
Jade ex Fondal-74, Gdansk-73	1967	1,498	287	43	12	M(A)
Olivine	1952	1,430	245	38	10½	M(A)
Sapphire	1966	1,286	228	37	12	M(A)
Topaz	1962	1,597	268	40	13	M(A)
Tourmaline	1962	1,581	268	40	13	M(A)
Kyle Shipping Co Ltd:						
Kylebank	1961	1,143	228	36	11	M(A)

See also Stephenson Clarke Ltd

R. L. ROGERS
(Celtic Ocean Salvage Co)

St. Ives

FUNNEL: Grey with black top.
HULL: Black with red boot-topping.

Name	Built	Tons	Length	Breadth	Speed	Engines
Salvage Vessel:						
Celtic Lord ex Seamoor-73, M.M.S.	1944	182	110	22	9	M

RONEZ LTD
(Huelin—Renouf Shipping Services)

Jersey

FUNNEL: Yellow with red letters "HL" on red bordered yellow diamond interrupting red bands.
HULL: Grey with red boot-topping.

Name	Built	Tons	Length	Breadth	Speed	Engines
Marshlea	1957	495	184	31	11	M(A)

C. ROWBOTHAM & SONS (MANAGEMENT) LTD

Farnborough

FUNNEL: Blue with black top with red letter "R" in white diamond.
HULL: Grey with blue boot-topping or black with red boot-topping.

Name	Built	Tons	Length	Breadth	Speed	Engines
Coastal Tankers:						
Anchorman	1962	795	203	31	10¾	M(A)
Astraman	1972	1,599	287	45	14	M(A)
Bridgeman	1972	3,701	340	50	13	M(A)
Chartsman	1967	787	203	31	10	M(A)
Guidesman	1964	799	203	31	10½	M(A)
Helmsman	1972	3,705	341	49	13	M(A)
Leadsman	1968	843	205	33	11	M(A)

C. Rowbotham & Sons (Management) Ltd (Continued)

Name	Built	Tons	Length	Breadth	Speed	Engines
New (3)	1976	3,550dw			13	M(A)
Pointsman	1970	2,886	325	47	12	M(A)
Polarisman	1972	1,599	287	45	14	M(A)
Quarterman	1973	1,226	239	36	11½	M(A)
Rudderman	1968	1,592	274	41	12	M(A)
Steersman	1970	1,567	274	41	12	M(A)
Tillerman	1963	807	203	31	10	M(A)
Wheelsman	1967	2,897	322	47	12¾	M(A)

SALVAGE & CABLE (FOLKESTONE) LTD

Folkestone

FUNNEL: Red with black top separated by yellow bordered blue diamond on yellow bordered blue band.
HULL: Grey with red boot-topping.

Name	Built	Tons	Length	Breadth	Speed	Engines
Salvage Vessel:						
Staley Bridge	1940	297	138	25	9	M(A)

CHRISTIAN SALVESEN (SHIPPING) LTD

Edinburgh

FUNNEL: Red with blue top separated by broad white band.
HULL: Black with red boot-topping.

Name	Built	Tons	Length	Breadth	Speed	Engines
Duncansby Head*	1969	4,440	369	52	12¾	M(A)
Dunvegan Head*	1968	4,485	362	52	12½	M(A)
Tod Head*	1971	1,599	284	39	12	M(A)
Troup Head*	1971	1,585	287	39	12	M(A)

* *In A. F. Henry & Macgregor colours*

Top: GEM, Wm. Robertson, Shipowners Ltd *J. Clarkson*

STEERSMAN, C. Rowbotham & Sons (Management) Ltd *J. Clarkson*

SAND SUPPLIES (WESTERN) LTD
(B. Silvey)

Bristol

FUNNEL: Black with dark blue letters "SS" superimposed on red bordered white letter "W" on broad white band, or variations.
HULL: Black with red boot-topping.

Name	Built	Tons	Length	Breadth	Speed	Engines
Sand Dredgers and Carriers:						
Sand Gem ex Jersey Castle-70, Wimborne-68	1949	313	147	25	9½	M(A)
Sand Jade ex Auriga G.-71, Auriga-54	1954	398	160	27	9½	M(A)
Sand Pearl ex Wycliffe-70	1949	113	100	18	8	M(A)
Sand Sapphire ex CY Threesome -74, Pass of Glenogle-73	1963	860	203	33	11½	M(A)
Sand Topaz ex Denby-70	1938	108	99	18	8	M(A)

SEA CONTAINERS LTD

London

FUNNEL & HULL: Usually those of the chartering company.

Name	Built	Tons	Length	Breadth	Speed	Engines
Delios	1973	1,592	288	45	15½	M(A)
Dorli	1973	1,592	288	45	15½	M(A)
Harp	1973	1,592	280	45	15	M(A)
Isbrit ex England-74	1970	1,578	280	45	16	M(A)
Londis ex Atlantic Bermudian-73	1971	1,593	284	45	15½	M(A)

Top: DUNCANSBY HEAD, Chris. Salvesen (Shipping) Ltd *F. R. Sherlock*

MINHO, Sea Containers Ltd *J. K. Byass*

Name	Built	Tons	Length	Breadth	Speed	Engines
Minho	1969	1,578	280	45	16	M(A)
Tagus	1970	1,598	280	45	16	M(A)
Tamega	1970	1,578	280	45	16	M(A)
Tiber	1970	1,599	280	45	15½	M(A)
Tormes	1970	1,578	280	45	16	M(A)
Tua	1970	1,599	280	45	16	M(A)
Vento di Maestrale	1971	1,593	285	45	15½	M(A)
Venti di Scirocco	1971	1,593	285	45	15½	M(A)
Voorloper ex Vento di Libeccio-71	1971	1,591	285	45	15½	M(A)
Sea Containers Chartering Ltd:						
Bergen Juno	1972	1,592	280	45	15½	M(A)
Britis ex Atlantic Jamaican-73	1971	1,590	280	45	15½	M(A)
Cheshire Endeavour ex Laula-73	1973	1592	280	45	15	M(A)
Cheshire Venture	1972	1,592	280	45	15	M(A)
Mondego	1972	1,598	280	45	15½	M(A)
Swift Arrow	1972	1,593	285	45	15	M(A)
Tronto	1971	1,578	279	45	16	M(A)
Union South Pacific	1973	1,594	280	45	15½	M(A)

SEA ISLAND MARINE LTD

Laleston, Nr. Bridgend

FUNNEL: Blue.
HULL: Dark grey with black boot-topping.

Name	Built	Tons	Length	Breadth	Speed	Engines
SIM Venture ex Polmear-74, David M.-73, Concorde-69, Rottum-65	1957	452	166	27	10	M(A)

SHAMROCK SHIPPING CO LTD
(C. S. Brown)

Larne

FUNNEL: Red with black top separated by blue band bearing white letter "S" but usually those of the chartering company.
HULL: Black with white Line and red boot-topping.

Name	Built	Tons	Length	Breadth	Speed	Engines
Curran	1967	1,325	229	36	12	M(A)
Moyle	1967	1,325	229	36	12	M(A)
OLIVE	1963	791	202	33	11	" "

Both vessels currently on charter to Atlantic Steam Navigation Co Ltd

H. K. SHAW

North Harrow

FUNNEL: Blue.
HULL: Black with grey topsides.

Name	Built	Tons	Length	Breadth	Speed	Engines
Fretherne ex Eagle 2-71, Merwestad-69, Favoriet-55, Campen-54	1950	351	147	23	8½	M(A)

SHAW SAVILL & ALBION CO LTD
(Furness Withy Group)

London

FUNNEL: Red with white triangle between narrow white bands separating black top (Cairn Line of Steamships Ltd colours), or those of chartering company.
HULL: Pale blue with red boot-topping.

Name	Built	Tons	Length	Breadth	Speed	Engines
Cairnranger	1971	1,598	287	39	12	M(A)
Cairnover	1971	1,598	287	39	12½	M(A)
Cairntrader ex Saxon Prince -74	1971	1,599	262	39	12	M(A)

Name	Built	Tons	Length	Breadth	Speed	Engines
Cairn Line of Steamships Ltd:						
New (7)	1974/77	3,200dw			13	M(A)

See also Prince Line Ltd

A. H. SHEAF & CO LTD

Newport, I.O.W.

FUNNEL: Yellow with white letters "ASH" on pale blue disc.
HULL: Grey with black boot-topping.

Name	Built	Tons	Length	Breadth	Speed	Engines
Ash Lake ex Dina-69, Mitropa-40	1939	201	126	22	9	M(A)

SHELL-MEX & BP LTD

London

FUNNEL: Black with yellow band between white bands.
HULL: Black, or black with red boot-topping.

Name	Built	Tons	Length	Breadth	Speed	Engines
Coastal Tankers:						
Ardrossan	1968	1,529	249	41	11	M(A)
B.P. Haulier	1955	315	148	29	7½	M(A)
Ben Harold						
Smith	1952	325	136	26	8½	M(A)
British Toiler	1925	131	109	23	7½	M(A)
Caernarvon	1971	1,210	217	40	11	M(A)

Shell-Mex & BP Ltd (Continued)

Name	Built	Tons	Length	Breadth	Speed	Engines
Dingle Bank	1966	1,177	216	37	10½	M(A)
Dublin	1969	1,077	215	37	11	M(A)
Dundee	1972	1,598	259	41	12	M(A)
Falmouth	1965	982	202	34	10½	M(A)
Grangemouth	1968	1,529	249	41	11	M(A)
Hamble	1964	1,182	215	37	10½	M(A)
Inverness	1968	1,542	249	41	11½	M(A)
Killingholme	1964	1,182	215	37	10½	M(A)
Pando	1968	647	171	35	9½	M(A)
Partington	1965	982	202	34	10½	M(A)
Perfecto	1967	652	172	35	9½	M(A)
Perso	1967	647	171	35	9½	M(A)
Plymouth	1972	1,210	217	40	11	M(A)
Poilo	1967	647	171	35	9½	M(A)
Point Law	1967	1,542	249	41	11	M(A)
Pronto	1967	652	172	35	9½	M(A)
Shell Dispenser	1963	239	133	27	9½	M(A)
Shell Farmer	1955	313	145	30	8	M(A)
Swansea	1972	1,598	259	41	12	M(A)
Teesport	1966	1,176	215	37	10½	M(A)
Torksey	1964	215	117	27	9½	M(A)
New	1974					M(A)
New	1974					M(A)

Coastal tankers of other companies also on charter

SHIPPING & COAL CO LTD

London

FUNNEL: Black with blue diamond on broad white band between narrow red bands.
HULL: Black with red boot-topping.

Name	Built	Tons	Length	Breadth	Speed	Engines
Greenland	1962	2,200	285	43	14½	M(A)
Highland ex Captain J. M. Donaldson-72	1951	3,341	339	46	10½	SR(A)
Queensland ex Greathope-64	1958	2,750	336	45	12	M(A)

SILLOTH SHIPPING CO LTD

Silloth

FUNNEL:
HULL: Black with red boot-topping.

Name	Built	Tons	Length	Breadth	Speed	Engines
Silloth Trader ex Rosemary D. -74, ex Valerie B.-73, Sarsfield- 70, Edgefield-65, Spolesto-56	1956	622	203	31	10½	M(A)

SILVER CHEMICAL TANKERS LTD

London

FUNNEL: Black with houseflag (White with blue panel containing two white diagonal stripes between narrow white bars).
HULL: Dark blue with red boot-topping.

Name	Built	Tons	Length	Breadth	Speed	Engines
Chemical Tankers:						
Silvereagle	1970	4,039	346	54	13½	M(A)
Silvereid	1969	1,596	300	40	13	M(A)
Silverfalcon	1966	1,301	254	41	12	M(A)
Silverkestrel	1965	456	186	31	12	M(A)
Silverosprey	1970	4,039	355	55	13¾	M(A)
Silverpelerin	1973	4,474	370	55	14	M(A)
John I. Jacobs & *Co Ltd:*						
Silvermerlin	1968	1,259	254	41	12	M(A)
Ship Mortgage *Finance Co Ltd:*						
Silverharrier	1970	4,622	346	54	13¾	M(A)

Top: MOYLE, Shamrock Shipping Co Ltd *J. Clarkson*

CAERNARVON, Shell-Mex & B.P. Ltd *J. K. Byass*

SOUTH WALES SAND & GRAVEL CO LTD
(L. G. Bevan)

Swansea

FUNNEL: White with houseflag on blue shield and narrow black top (Houseflag; red with white letter "B" and white pole).
HULL: Black with red boot-topping.

Name	Built	Tons	Length	Breadth	Speed	Engines
Sand Dredgers and Carriers:						
Glen Gower	1963	552	169	30	10	M(A)
Glen Hafod	1960	552	169	30	10	M(A)

SOUTHAMPTON, ISLE OF WIGHT & SOUTH OF ENGLAND ROYAL MAIL STEAM PACKET CO LTD

Southampton

FUNNEL: Red with black top and Company symbol in red and white on superstructure.
HULL: Black with red boot-topping.

Name	Built	Tons	Length	Breadth	Speed	Engines
Isle of Wight Ferries:						
Carisbrooke Castle	1959	672	191	42	14	M(2)
Cowes Castle	1965	786	191	42	14	M(2)
Netley Castle	1973	1,188	225			M(F & A)
Norris Castle	1968	734	191	42	14	M(2)
Osborne Castle	1962	736	191	42	14	M(2)

See also Tugs

SOUTHERN TANKER & BUNKERING CO LTD

Southampton

FUNNEL: Yellow with houseflag (Yellow letters "STBC" in each corner of blue field with black "&" in white diamond between black edged white bands).
HULL: Dark grey or black with red boot-topping, or black.

Name	Built	Tons	Length	Breadth	Speed	Engines
Coastal and Bunkering Tankers:						
Clydestan ex Kai-73	1968	457	205	30	$11\frac{1}{4}$	M(A)
Easternstan ex Wyesdale H.-70	1951	234	137	21	8	M(A)
Northernstan ex Northdale H.-71	1950	172	124	18	8	M(A)
Southernstan ex Shell Roadbuilder-70	1956	303	139	22	8	M(A)
Westernstan ex Westerndale H.-68	1947	220	135	21	$8\frac{1}{2}$	M(A)

STEPHENSON CLARKE SHIPPING LTD

London

FUNNEL: Black with broad silver band.
HULL: Black with white topline and red boot-topping.

Name	Built	Tons	Length	Breadth	Speed	Engines
Angmering ex Rattrey Head-73	1965	1,600	247	43	$10\frac{1}{2}$	M(A)
Ashington ex Tennyson-68	1957	3,894	357	50	11	M(A)
Beeding	1971	1,595	285	42	12	M(A)
Birling* ex Thomas Hardie-68	1950	1,771	271	40	10	M(A)
Climping ex Camberwell-69	1958	1,877	275	39	11	M(A)
Cowdray	1959	1,784	245	40	11	M(A)
Ferring	1969	1,596	285	43	$12\frac{1}{2}$	M(A)
Fletching* ex Ewell-70	1958	1,877	275	39	11	M(A)

* Thames "Up-river" or "Flat-iron" Collie

Stephenson Clarke Shipping Ltd (Continued)

Name	Built	Tons	Length	Breadth	Speed	Engines
Harting* ex Thomas Livesey-69	1953	1,779	271	40	10	M(A)
Jevington ex Macauley-68	1959	5,330	414	55	12½	M(A)
Keynes* ex Accum-67	1950	1,771	271	40	11	M(A)
Lancing	1958	1,765	262	38	10½	M(A)
Malling	1969	1,596	285	43	12½	M(A)
Portslade	1955	1,937	242	40	11	M(A)
Pulborough	1965	4,995	370	53	12½	M(A)
Rogate	1967	4,997	370	53	12½	M(A)
Shoreham	1957	1,834	262	40	12	M(A)
Steyning ex Glanton-71	1965	1,594	269	35	12	M(A)
Storrington	1959	3,809	345	49	11	M(A)
Tarring* ex Lambeth-70	1958	1,877	275	39	11	M(A)
Totland	1952	1,570	241	38	11½	M(A)
Wadhurst ex Saphir-70	1962	3,819	375	49	12	M(A)
Wilmington	1969	5,689	410	55	13	M(A)
Worthing* ex Dulwich-70	1957	1,873	275	39	11	M(A)
New (2)	1975/76	11,000dw			12	M(A)
Coastal Tankers:						
Ashurst	1964	3,451	366	51	12½	M(A)
Fernhurst	1961	1,473	260	40	10½	M(A)
Firle	1958	948	211	35	9	M(A)
Friston	1959	948	211	34	9½	M(A)
Maplehurst	1961	1,476	253	40	10¼	M(A)
Midhurst	1960	1,473	260	40	10¼	M(A)
Petworth	1958	1,266	234	35	10½	M(A)
Hopper Barges, *Sludge Carriers,* *etc:*						
Adderstone ex Springwood- 72	1950	814	185	36	11¾	M(A)
David Marley	1963	730	182	37	9½	M(A)
Falstone ex Amsterdam VI	1934	359	131	27	8½	M(A)
Megstone† ex Cargo Fleet No. 3-72	1946	988	207	35	8½	SR(A)

* *Thames "Up-river" or "Flat-iron" Colliers*

† *Laid up. See also William Robertson, Shipowners, Ltd*

Top: SOUTHERNSTAN, Southern Tanker & Bunkering Co Ltd *F. R. Sherlock*

MALLING, Stephenson Clarke Shipping Ltd *F. R. Sherlock*

SULLY FREIGHT

London

FUNNEL: Black with red letter "S" on white disc on green band between narrow white bands.
HULL: Green with black boot-topping.

Name	Built	Tons	Length	Breadth	Speed	Engines
Subro Venture	1971	196	100	23	8	M(A)

RAYMOND A. SULLY & L. G. STREVENS

Sittingbourne

FUNNEL: None.
HULL: Black.

Name	Built	Tons	Length	Breadth	Speed	Engines
Hydrogen	1906	124	94	22	7	M(2)(A)
Peter Robin ex Admiralty X-Lighter	1916	156	105	21	$7\frac{1}{2}$	M(A)
Trilby	1896	153	96	23	$7\frac{3}{4}$	M(2)(A)

SUTTON'S INTERNATIONAL LTD

London

FUNNEL: Pale blue with company symbol.
HULL: Pale blue with red boot-topping.

Name	Built	Tons	Length	Breadth	Speed	Engines
Slop and Sullage Tanker:						
John S. Darbyshire ex Edwharf-74, Esso Jersey-73	1961	300	123	24	9	M(A)

TARMAC SHIPPING CO LTD
(Tarmac Roadstone Holdings Ltd)

Middlesbrough

FUNNEL: Khaki green with Company symbol in black and white and black top.
HULL:

Name	Built	Tons	Length	Breadth	Speed	Engines
Tarmac I ex Alletta-73	1956	498	193	30	9½	M(A)

TAYLOR WOODROW CONSTRUCTION LTD

London

FUNNEL: Black with four red "men" on broad white band.
HULL: Black with red boot-topping.

Name	Built	Tons	Length	Breadth	Speed	Engines
Teamwork ex Warlight-72, Leaspray-66, Goldeve	1932	199	96	23	8½	M(A)

See also Harbour Works and Dredging Craft section

R. TAYLOR & SONS (SCRAP) LTD

Bury

FUNNEL: Green with orange Cross of Lorraine supported in orange ring.
HULL: Grey with black boot-topping.

Name	Built	Tons	Length	Breadth	Speed	Engines
Ravenstonedale ex Colpro Adventurer-73, Isola-73	1954	397	162	27	10	M(A)

TEXACO OVERSEAS TANKSHIPS LTD

London

FUNNEL: Black with "TEXACO" badge on broad green band.
HULL: Black with red boot-topping.

Name	Built	Tons	Length	Breadth	Speed	Engines
Coastal Tankers:						
Texaco .Whitegate ex Caltex Whitegate-66, Caltex Pakenbaru-59	1952	2,022	260	45	11	M(2)(A)
Texaco Gloucester* ex Regent Eagle-69	1959	12,834	571	72	14	M(A)

* *Former Ocean Tanker*

THAMES SERVICES (MARINE) LTD

Tilbury

FUNNEL: White with black top separated by broad blue band.
HULL: Black with red boot-topping or blue with black boot-topping.

Name	Built	Tons	Length	Breadth	Speed	Engines
Tairlaw ex Tim-67, Walcheren	1941	187	123	22	9	M(A)
Tremont ex Lady Sabina-73, Glencullen-68, Walcheren-64	1952	410	149	24	9	M(A)
Thames Welding Co Ltd: (*White letters "TW" on blue band*)						
Tank Cleaning Vessel:						
Tanklean						

See also Tugs

TOWER MARIE, Tower Shipping Ltd *J. Clarkson*

W. F. THOMPSON

Ipswich

FUNNEL: White with red top.
HULL: Black.

Name	Built	Tons	Length	Breadth	Speed	Engines
Polythene	1949	330	140	25	9	M(A)

R. J. TODD

Portsmouth

FUNNEL: None.
HULL: Grey with black boot-topping.

Name	Built	Tons	Length	Breadth	Speed	Engines
Regent Swift	1952	105	91	19	7	M(A)

* Fitted with bow lift and for diving.

TOWER SHIPPING LTD

London

FUNNEL: Blue with white tower device.
HULL: Grey with black boot-topping.

Name	Built	Tons	Length	Breadth	Speed	Engines
Tower Conquest	1968	200	137	25	9	M(A)
Tower Duchess	1969	200	137	25	9	M(A)
Tower Helen ✓	1971	425	157	29	9½	M(A)
Tower Julie ✓	1972	499	183	33	10	M(A)
Tower Marie	1969	199	137	26	9	M(A)
Tower Princess	1969	200	137	25	9	M(A)
Tower Venture	1968	200	137	25	9	M(A)

Fordham Navigation: (Funnel: Blue with large red bordered company symbol in white.)

Name	Built	Tons	Length	Breadth	Speed	Engines
Fordonna	1972	499	183	32	10	M(A)

TOWNSEND CAR FERRIES LTD
(European Ferries Ltd)

Dover

FUNNEL: Red with green "TTF" monogram.
HULL: Light green with red boot-topping.

Name	Built	Tons	Length	Breadth	Speed	Engines
Free Enterprise I ex Free Enterprise-64	1962	2,607	316	54	18	M(2)
Free Enterprise IV	1969	5,049	385	64	20¾	M(3)
Free Enterprise V	1970	5,044	386	64	20¾	M(3)
Free Enterprise VI	1972	5,050	386	64	21	M(3)
Free Enterprise VII	1972	4,980	386	64	21	M(3)
New (7)	1974/75	6,000			18½	M(3)
Stanhope Steamship Co Ltd:						
Free Enterprise II	1965	4,011	355	60	19	M(2)
Free Enterprise III	1966	4,657	385	63	20	M(2)
Operated by P. & A. Campbell Ltd, Bristol. (Funnel: white, Hull: black with white line and red boot-topping)						
Balmoral	1949	688	204	32	14½	M(2)

See also Atlantic Steam Navigation Co Ltd

TRIPORT SHIPPING CO LTD

London

FUNNEL: White with black wheel and blue wave device.
HULL: Blue with red boot-topping.

Name	Built	Tons	Length	Breadth	Speed	Engines
Car & Vehicle Ferries:						
Tor Belgia	1972	4,128	451	69	18½	M(2)(A)
Tor Gothia ✔	1971	4,128	451	69	18½	M(2)(A)
Tor Mercia	1969	1,600	356	64	12	M(2)(A)
Tor Nerlandia	1972	4,128	451	69	18½	M(2)(A)
Tor Scandia	1970	1,600	360	64	12	M(2)(A)
New (2)	1975	13,500			26	M(2)
New	1976	13,500			26	M(2)

TRUCKLINE FERRIES LTD

Poole

FUNNEL: Dark grey.
HULL: Yellow with blue boot-topping.

Name	Built	Tons	Length	Breadth	Speed	Engines
Vehicle Ferries:						
Dauphine de Cherbourg*	1973	700	246	50	13	M(2)
Poole Antelope	1973	700	246	50	13	M(2)

* French flag

TURNBULL, SCOTT MANAGEMENT LTD

Farnborough

FUNNEL: Black with white letters "TS" in white bordered red shield.
HULL: Black with red boot-topping.

Name	Built	Tons	Length	Breadth	Speed	Engines
Turnbull, Scott Shipping Ltd:						
Eskdalegate ex Fredericksgate -74, Bruni-74	1969	2,889	316	48	14	M(A)
Highgate	1972	1,599	287	39	11½	M(A)
Redgate	1968	1,426	254	39	11¼	M(A)
Saltersgate	1968	1,426	253	39	11¼	M(A)
Waynegate	1971	1,600	278	43	12	M(A)
Whitegate	1972	1,600	287	39	12	M(A)
New (2)	1975/76	5,700dw	312	51	14	M(A)
Chemical Tanker:						
New	1975	3,500dw	—	—	13½	M(A)
Park Steamships Ltd. (Funnel: Dark green with white "PS" monogram. Hull: Grey with red boot-topping)						
Norrstal	1972	1,599	287	39	11½	M(A)
Regent's Park	1972	1,600	285	39	11½	M(A)
Syon Park	1973					M(A)
Tere	1970	1,598	276	39	12¾	M(A)
New	1976	5,700dw	312	51	14	M(A)

Turnbull, Scott Management Ltd (Continued)

Name	Built	Tons	Length	Breadth	Speed	Engines
Whitehall Shipping Co Ltd. (Funnel: Yellow. Hull: Grey with red boot-topping.)						
Coastal Oil/Chemical Tankers:						
Stainless Duke	1972	1,561	285	40	13	M(A)
Stainless Patriot	1973	1,599	285	40	13	M(A)
Stainless Warrior	1970	1,599	285	40	12	M(A)

TYNE TEES DISPOSAL CO LTD
Middlesbrough

FUNNEL:
HULL:　　　Black with red boot-topping.

Name	Built	Tons	Length	Breadth	Speed	Engines
Effluent Tanker:						
Onward Enterprise ex Dago 2-66, Dago II-66, Mathea-63	1960	334	159	27	10	M(A)

TYNE-TEES STEAM SHIPPING CO LTD
(P & O Group)

Newcastle

FUNNEL:　Black with white over red bands or those of the chartering company.
HULL:　　　Black with white line and red boot-topping.

Name	Built	Tons	Length	Breadth	Speed	Engines
Norbank* ex Bison-71	1962	1,343	258	42	14	M(A)
Roe Deer† ex Norbrae-73, Buffalo-72	1962	1,482	258	43	14	M(A)
Stormont ex Fruin-63, Fife Coast-58	1954	906	226	36	12	M(A)

* Charter to MacAndrews & Co Ltd

† Chartered to European Unit Routes

See also Belfast Steamship Co Ltd, General Steam Navigation (Trading) Ltd, North of Scotland Orkney & Shetland Shipping Co Ltd and North Sea Ferries Ltd

UML LTD
(Unilever Ltd.)

Bebington, Cheshire

FUNNEL: Yellow with green top.
HULL: Green.

Name	Built	Tons	Length	Breadth	Speed	Engines
Laundola	1947	189	100	23	8	M(A)
Lifebuoy	1949	198	101	23	8½	M(A)
Lobol	1941	200	101	23	8½	M(A)
Lux	1950	205	100	23	8½	M(A)
Rinso	1947	198	101	23	8½	M(A)

See also Harbour Works & Dredging Craft.

UNITED BALTIC CORPORATION LTD

London

FUNNEL: Pale yellow with narrow black top and houseflag device on black edged white disc.
HULL: Grey with green boot-topping.

Name	Built	Tons	Length	Breadth	Speed	Engines
Baltic Arrow	1956	1,385	291	41	14½	M(2)
Baltic Progress	1973	4,668	451	73	18	M(2)(A)
Baltic Star	1961	2,853	305	42	14	M(A)
Baltic Valiant	1969	2,125	339	52	14	M(A)
Baltic Vanguard	1966	1,785	308	49	15	M(A)
Baltic Venture	1965	1,844	322	46	13½	M(2)
Baltic Viking	1967	1,599	245	41	14	M(A)
Anglo Finnish Shipping Co Ltd:						
Baltic Enterprise	1973	4,668	451	73	18	M(2)(A)
Baltic Jet	1959	1,481	299	42	14	M(A)

USBORNE & SONS (LONDON) LTD

London

FUNNEL: White with black letter "U" in red ring or red with black top and white letter "U".
HULL: Grey with black boot-topping.

Name	Built	Tons	Length	Breadth	Speed	Engines
Carnoustie ex Osteland-73, Wilpo-69	1960	495	184	30	10	M(A)
Hoylake ex Warstade-74, Jenny Porr-69, Brosund-62	1961	1,543	270	36	15½	M(A)
Portmarnock ex Shevrell-73, Wirral Coast-72	1962	881	203	36	12	M(A)
St. Andrews ex Johanne-72	1961	437	172	29	9¾	M(A)
Turnberry ex Lieselotte Flint-73, Roodebeek-69	1966	424	174	27	9¼	M(A)
Buries Markes Ltd:						
Birkdale ex Herma Martens-73	1965	499	206	31	10	M(A)
Thornby Grain Ltd:						
Ganton ex Uloe-74	1961	424	171	29	9¾	M(A)

VAN BROEK MARINE (SHIPPING) LTD

Twickenham

FUNNEL: Yellow with white "VB" monogram on inverted blue triangle interrupting two black bands.
HULL: Grey with black boot-topping.

Name	Built	Tons	Length	Breadth	Speed	Engines
Georgena B. ex Oldambt-71	1949	224	132	21	9	M(A)
Ivy B. ex Caravelle-72, Delfdijk-64	1956	350	148	25	8	M(A)

Van Broek Marine (Shipping) Ltd (Continued)

Name	Built	Tons	Length	Breadth	Speed	Engines
H. Taylor & Son (Isleworth) Ltd:						
Doreen B. ex Forel-73	1956	350	148	25	8	M(A)

VECTIS SHIPPING CO LTD

Newport, I.O.W.

FUNNEL: Yellow with red letters "VSC".
HULL: Grey with yellow line and black boot-topping.

Name	Built	Tons	Length	Breadth	Speed	Engines
Murius	1962	125	97	20	8	M(2)(A)
Newclose	1960	118	98	20	7	M(2)(A)
Riverclose	1957	110	90	20	8	M(2)(A)

THOMAS WATSON (SHIPPING) LTD

Rochester

FUNNEL: Yellow with blue band between red bands.
HULL: Blue with black boot-topping.

Name	Built	Tons	Length	Breadth	Speed	Engines
Lady Sandra	1970	199	137	25	9	M(A)
Lady Sarita	1965	200	136	25	9	M(A)
Lady Serena	1964	200	137	25	8¾	M(A)
Lady Sheena	1966	200	136	25	9	M(A)
Downlands Shipping Inc (Liberian flag):						
Lady Sophia ex Shannon-70	1964	596	214	32	13	M(A)
Andrean Shipping Ltd (Cyprus flag):						
Lady Sabina ex Cellona-74, Pirje-70	1962	1,923	282	41	13	M(A)

Thomas Watson (Shipping) Ltd (Continued)

Name	Built	Tons	Length	Breadth	Speed	Engines
Lady Sylvia ex Lienersand-72	1965	1,000	230	37	11½	M(A)

See also G. E. Gray & Sons (Shipping) Ltd

B. W. WELLS

Chatham

FUNNEL: None.
HULL: Grey with black boot-topping.

Name	Built	Tons	Length	Breadth	Speed	Engines
Celtic	1903	153	90	23	7	M(2)(A)

WESTERN DREDGERS LTD

Swansea

FUNNEL: Yellow with black top and houseflag.
HULL: Black with red boot-topping.

Name	Built	Tons	Length	Breadth	Speed	Engines
Sand Dredgers and Carriers:						
Instow	1964	735	186	34	9½	M(A)
Isca	1960	550	170	30	9	M(A)
Moderator	1965	836	195	37	10	M(A)

WESTERN FERRIES LTD
(Dornoch Shipping Co Ltd)
(Lithgow (Holdings))

Glasgow

FUNNEL: White with red wheel and arrow device on superstructure, or blue with red wheel and arrow device on white disc.
HULL: Red.

Name	Built	Tons	Length	Breadth	Speed	Engines
Car and Vehicle Ferries:						
Sound of Ghia	1965	176	95	22	10	M(2)(A)
Sound of Islay*	1968	280	143	31	10¾	M(2)
Sound of Jura	1969	519	162	36	14	M(2)
Sound of Sanda ex Lymington-74	1938	275	148	37	9	M
Dornoch Shipping Co Ltd, Campbeltown:						
Sound of Scarba ex Olandssund III-73	1960	245	138	30	10	M(F & A)
Sound of Shuna ex Olandssund IV-73	1962	243	138	30	10	M(F & A)

* *Chartered to Outer Isles Containers Ltd*

WESTERN SHIPPING LTD

Plymouth

FUNNEL: Blue with white and blue letters "WS" on blue and white diamond on broad white band.
HULL: Blue with red boot-topping.

Name	Built	Tons	Length	Breadth	Speed	Engines
Treviscoe ex Lijnbaans-gracht-62	1952	494	172	28	10½	M(A)

WESTMINSTER GRAVELS LTD

Southampton

FUNNEL: White with black top and houseflag (Divided diagonally yellow over blue).
HULL: Black or grey with red boot-topping.

Name	Built	Tons	Length	Breadth	Speed	Engines
Sand Dredgers and Carriers:						
Bankstone ex Hydracrete-63 Poole Island-59	1949	1,357	235	36	9½	M(A)
Norstone ex Konsul Retzlaff-70	1964	1,599	276	39	12	M(A)
Rockstone ex James No. 47-64, P.L.A. Hopper No. 8, Thames Conservancy Hopper No. 8	1907	842	204	32	9	M(A)
Wightstone ex Brentford-61, Brent Knoll-61	1950	1,313	235	36	9¼	M(A)

J. WHARTON (SHIPPING) LTD

Gunness

FUNNEL: Black with black letter "W" on red diamond on broad yellow band.
HULL: Black with blue top line and red boot-topping.

Name	Built	Tons	Length	Breadth	Speed	Engines
Brendonia	1966	604	177	30	10	M(A)
Gladonia	1963	658	186	30	10	M(A)
Trent Lighterage Ltd:						
Ecctonia	1963	658	186	30	10	M(A)
Trentonia	1964	604	177	30	10½	M(A)

JOHN H. WHITAKER (HOLDING) LTD

Hull

FUNNEL: White with houseflag on narrow red over black over narrow green bands.
HULL: Grey with red boot-topping.

Name	Built	Tons	Length	Breadth	Speed	Engines
Coastal Tanker:						
Whitonia ex Axel-70	1965	422	182	28	10½	M(A)

Many smaller tank barges on various inland and estuaral waters

J. WIEGMAN SHIPPING CO LTD

London

FUNNEL: Blue with black top (On charter to European Unit Routes).
HULL: Blue with red boot-topping and white "EUR" midships.

Name	Built	Tons	Length	Breadth	Speed	Engines
Sassaby √	1971	499	253	42	13	M(A)

P. E. & F. C. WIELAND

Ipswich

FUNNEL: White with red top.
HULL: Black.

Name	Built	Tons	Length	Breadth	Speed	Engines
Wall Brook	1940	244	130	25	8	M(A)

SASSABY, J. Wiegman Shipping Co Ltd *F. R. Sherlock*

WILLIAMS SHIPPING CO (FAWLEY) LTD

Southampton

FUNNEL: Black with houseflag on orange band.
HULL: Black with orange line and red boot-topping with white line.

Name	Built	Tons	Length	Breadth	Speed	Engines
Wilbernie	1960	125	97	20	7½	M(A)
Wilclair	1935	124	91	19	7½	M(A)
ex Severn Industry-62						
Wilmere	1930	134	98	20	7½	M(A)

J. WILLMENT (MARINE) LTD

Twickenham

FUNNEL: Yellow.
HULL: Yellow.

Name	Built	Tons	Length	Breadth	Speed	Engines
Sand Dredgers and Carriers:						
Sand Robin	1950	116	91	19	7	M(A)
ex Regent Robin-67						
Bedhampton Sand & Gravel Co Ltd:						
Hexhamshire Lass	1955	561	158	33	10½	M(A)
Woodford (London) Ltd:						
Mersey Beaucoup	1957	637	167	36	10	M(A)
Paull Holme	1961	900	192	40	9	M(A)

See also Tugs

WINDLE SHIPPING CO LTD
(Vogt & Maguire Ltd)

Liverpool

FUNNEL: Blue with white "VM" Monogram.
HULL: Black with red boot-topping.

Name	Built	Tons	Length	Breadth	Speed	Engines
Windle Sea ex Kalmarborg-74, Lina-70, Virna-66	1963	1,548	260	40	11	M(A)
Windle Sky ex Cap Falcon-73, Lis Frellsen-67	1962	1,510	260	39	12	M(A)

N. W. WOODS

Gosport

FUNNEL: None.
HULL: Black.

Name	Built	Tons	Length	Breadth	Speed	Engines
Sand Dredger and Carrier: **Shell Mex No. 3**	1916	128	106	22	5	M(A)

WYVERN MARITIME LTD
(Ashmead (Padstow) Ltd)

Padstow

FUNNEL: Black with red outlined "Wyvern" on broad white band.
HULL: Black, or black with red boot-topping.

Name	Built	Tons	Length	Breadth	Speed	Engines
Sand Dredgers and Carriers:						
Field	1949	133	81	20	8	M(A)
Sand Wyvern ex Sand Grebe-73	1959	531	174	30	9	DE(A)

IRISH REPUBLIC

ALLIED IRISH BANKS LTD
Dublin

FUNNEL & HULL: Leased to British & Irish Steam Packet Co Ltd and operating in their colours.

Name	Built	Tons	Length	Breadth	Speed	Engines
Vehicle Ferry:						
Dundalk	1974	2,500				M(2)(A)
Container Ship:						
Kilkenny	1973	1,514	325	53	15	M(A)

AVOCA SHIPPING LTD
(Arrow Services)
Dublin

FUNNEL: Green with black and yellow company device on orange octagonal panel supporting white band.
HULL: Black with red boot-topping.

Name	Built	Tons	Length	Breadth	Speed	Engines
Kilcrea ex Fritz Raabe-70 Maria Althoff-57	1951	409	161	25	9	M(A)

BETSON SHIPPING CO LTD
Dublin

FUNNEL: Yellow with narrow black top and very broad white band between narrow black bands.
HULL: Grey with black boot-topping.

Name	Built	Tons	Length	Breadth	Speed	Engines
Quo Vadis	1956	492	170	28	9	M(A)
Quo Vadimus ex Hein Sietas -74	1961	382	169	27	10	M(A)

BRITISH & IRISH STEAM PACKET CO LTD
(Irish Government State Line)

Dublin

FUNNEL: White with black top and company device in red.
HULL: Blue with green boot-topping.

Name	Built	Tons	Length	Breadth	Speed	Engines
Passenger and Vehicle Ferries:						
Innisfallen	1969	4,849	388	59	21	M(2)
Leinster	1969	4,849	388	59	21	M(2)
Munster	1968	4,067	361	58	21	M(2)
Container Ship:						
Wicklow	1971	3,422	367	53	15	M(A)

The Company also employ Irish and foreign flag tonnage on charter

CELTIC COASTERS LTD

Dublin

FUNNEL: Black with diagonal green bands on broad white band, or * Black with company device in blue and green on white band.
HULL: Grey with red boot-topping.

Name	Built	Tons	Length	Breadth	Speed	Engines
Coastal and Estuaral Tankers:						
Breeda J.	1952	422	165	27	9	M(A)
ex Regent Jane-67						
Celtic 3	1956	301	139	22	8	M(A)
ex BP Miller-71						
Mary J.	1955	754	196	35	10	M(A)
ex Esso Poole-68						
Rathdown*	1965	1,409	253	39	11	M(A)
ex Thorheide-70, Mikhal-67						
Rathgar*	1959	965	217	32	11½	M(A)
ex Pass of Kildrummy-70						
Clondusc Partnership:						
Rathowen	1963	498	204	31	11½	M(A)
ex Bellona-74, Thuntank 10-67						

Celtic Coasters Ltd (Continued)

Name	Built	Tons	Length	Breadth	Speed	Engines
Dublin Shipping Ltd:						
Rathmines* ex Stanstead-72	1957	1,034	223	34	10½	M(A)

COMMERCIAL FERRIES LTD
(Hellenic Shipping & Trading Co Ltd)

Dublin

FUNNEL: Blue with yellow letters "CF" or charterers colours.
HULL: Blue with red boot-topping.

Name	Built	Tons	Length	Breadth	Speed	Engines
Celtic Trader ex Saskia-73, Fivel-70	1952	498	168	27	9½	M(A)
Hellenic Shipping and Trading Co Ltd:						
Howth Trader ex Hawthorn-74, Harglen-68, Irish Heather-64	1952	1,054	217	35	11	M(A)

Also the Panamanian vessels;

Diamond Trader, 353/56; Corinthian Trader 1,216/55; Ocean Trader, 1,110/58; Lancaster Trader, 949/55

CORAS IOMPAIR EIREANN
(Irish Transport System)

Galway

FUNNEL: Red with company's winged wheel device in white between narrow white bands.
HULL: Orange.

Name	Built	Tons	Length	Breadth	Speed	Engines
Ferry:						

Top: RIVER AVOCA, R.V.T. Hall *J. Clarkson*

SAINT PATRICK, Irish Continental Line *V. Barford*

Coras Iompair Eireann (Continued)

Name	Built	Tons	Length	Breadth	Speed	Engines
Naom Eanna (Saint Enda)	1958	483	137	28	9	M(A)

Aran Islands Ferry service

GALWAY FERRIES LTD

Galway

FUNNEL: Green with green letters "GFL" on white band.
HULL: Black with red boot-topping.

Name	Built	Tons	Length	Breadth	Speed	Engines
Ferry: **Galway Bay** ex Calshot-64	1930	702	148	33	13	M

Chartered to Coras Iompair Eireann for Aran Islands Service

GREENORE FERRY SERVICES LTD

Greenore

FUNNEL: Orange with green top separated by white band with "GFS" device in black and green.
HULL: Grey with blue boot-topping.

Name	Built	Tons	Length	Breadth	Speed	Engines
Irish Coast* ex Owenglas-71	1970	763	257	39	13½	M(A)
Mulcair	1958	480	194	30	11	M(A)
Owenbawn ex Lady Sanchia-68, Alfonso-66	1950	841	247	37	13	M(A)

* *Chartered to Coast Lines (P & O Group) and operating in their colours*
The Company also employ foreign flag tonnage on charter

ARTHUR GUINNESS, SON & CO (DUBLIN) LTD

Dublin

FUNNEL: Red with black top.
HULL: Blue with white line and red boot-topping.

Name	Built	Tons	Length	Breadth	Speed	Engines
The Lady Grania	1952	1,152	213	36	11	M(A)
The Lady Gwendolen	1953	1,166	213	36	11	M(A)
Stout Tanker:						
The Lady Patricia	1962	1,385	213	38	11	M(A)

The ships sail under the British flag

R. V. T. HALL

Arklow

FUNNEL: Green with black top and green "HT" monogram on black edged white panel.
HULL: Green with black boot-topping.

Name	Built	Tons	Length	Breadth	Speed	Engines
River Avoca ex Stevonia-62	1948	384	148	25	9	M(A)

IRISH CONTINENTAL LINE LTD
(Irish Shipping Ltd.—Managers)

Dublin

FUNNEL: Yellow with houseflag (Cross of Saint Patrick with Fleur de Lys superimposed) superimposed on green over white over blue bands.
HULL: White with red boot-topping.

Name	Built	Tons	Length	Breadth	Speed	Engines
Passenger & Vehicle Ferry:						
Saint Patrick	1973	5,465	387	60	21	M(2)

IRISH SEA OPERATORS LTD

Dublin

FUNNEL: In colours of charterer.
HULL: Blue with green boot-topping.

Name	Built	Tons	Length	Breadth	Speed	Engines
Kerry	1971	787	245	43	14	M(A)
Sligo	1971	787	245	43	14	M(A)

GEORGE KEARON LTD

Arklow

FUNNEL: Green with orange letter "K" in white edged green diamond with or without black top.
HULL: Black with red boot-topping.

Name	Built	Tons	Length	Breadth	Speed	Engines
New	1975	1,500dw				M(A)

LIVEOX SHIPPING LTD

Dublin

FUNNEL: Orange over green with black top and large white disc.
HULL: White.

Name	Built	Tons	Length	Breadth	Speed	Engines
Livestock Carrier:						
Liveox ex Sinjoor-73, Maria-67	1959	952	270	38	13½	M(A)

MARINE TRANSPORT SERVICES LTD

Cobb

FUNNEL: Pale blue with red top.
HULL: Black with red boot-topping.

Name	Built	Tons	Length	Breadth	Speed	Engines
Celt ex Fishersvic-54, Vic 64-48	1946	139	85	20	7½	M(A)
Corpach ex Vic 95-50	1945	141	85	20	7½	M(A)
Glenbrook ex Arklow Vale- 72, Torquay-72, Roscrea-64	1963	443	167	27	11	M(A)
Marloag ex Margareta B.-74	1966	379	159	28	9	M(A)
The Miller	1932	118	90	19	7	M(2)(A)

SHELBOURNE SHIPOWNING CO

Dublin

FUNNEL & HULL: Charterers colours.

Name	Built	Tons	Length	Breadth	Speed	Engines
Kildare	1968	622	256	45	12	M(A)
Tipperary	1969	622	256	44	12	M(A)

SHROVE SHIPPING LTD
(Capt. Neil Gillespie)

Dublin

FUNNEL: Yellow with black top and broad white band.
HULL: Grey with black boot-topping/between narrow black bands.

Name	Built	Tons	Length	Breadth	Speed	Engines
Tramone ex Paul Westers -74	1955	473	169	28	9½	M(A)

JAMES TYRRELL LTD

Arklow

FUNNEL: Yellow with broad white band between narrow green bands.
HULL: Green with red boot-topping or * blue with red boot-topping.

Name	Built	Tons	Length	Breadth	Speed	Engines
Darell	1970	387	148	28	11	M(A)
Murell	1974	945	200	32	11	M(A)
Bay Shipping Ltd:						
Arklow Dawn ✓	1973	943	200	32	11	M(A)

MICHAEL G. TYRRELL

Arklow

FUNNEL: Green with orange letter "T" in white triangle.
HULL: Black with green boot-topping.

Name	Built	Tons	Length	Breadth	Speed	Engines
Joan T. ex Thomas M.-73, Scheldt-70	1959	397	153	25	10	M(A)

PILOT, LIGHTHOUSE AND BUOY TENDERS

CLYDE PORT AUTHORITY

Glasgow

FUNNEL: Yellow with black top.
HULL: Blue with red boot-topping.

Name	Built	Tons	Length	Breadth	Speed	Engines
Buoy Vessel:						
Torch	1924	329	137	27	10½	SR(2)

See also Harbour Works and Dredging Craft

COMMISSIONERS OF IRISH LIGHTS

Dublin

FUNNEL: Yellow.
HULL: Grey with red boot-topping separated by white line.

Name	Built	Tons	Length	Breadth	Speed	Engines
Lighthouse Tenders:						
Atlanta	1959	1,185	213	38	14	DE(2)
Granuaile	1970	2,003	265	43	14	M(2)
Isolda	1953	1,173	233	38	12½	SR(2)

COMMISSIONERS OF NORTHERN LIGHTHOUSES

Leith

FUNNEL: Yellow-brown.
HULL: Black with white line and red boot-topping.

Name	Built	Tons	Length	Breadth	Speed	Engines
Lighthouse Tenders:						

Name	Built	Tons	Length	Breadth	Speed	Engines
Fingal	1964	1,342	239	40	13½	M(2)
Pharos	1955	1,712	257	40	14	M(2)
Pole Star	1961	1,328	236	40	14	M(2)

MERSEY DOCKS & HARBOUR CO

Liverpool

FUNNEL: Yellow with black top.
HULL: Black with white line and red boot-topping.

Name	Built	Tons	Length	Breadth	Speed	Engines
Pilot Tenders:						
Arnet Robinson	1958	734	177	32	11	M(2)
Edmund Gardner	1953	617	177	32	11	M(2)
Sir Thomas Brocklebank	1950	675	175	32	11	M(2)
Salvage and Buoy Vessels:						
Salvor	1947	671	173	35	12½	SR(2)
Vigilant	1953	728	173	35	12½	SR(2)

See also Harbour Works & Dredging Craft

CORPORATION OF TRINITY HOUSE

London

FUNNEL: Yellow.
HULL: Black with white line and red boot-topping.

Name	Built	Tons	Length	Breadth	Speed	Engines
Lighthouse Tenders:						
Argus	1948	1,918	267	40	12	SR(2)
Mermaid	1959	1,425	221	38	12½	DE(2)
Ready ✓	1947	1,920	267	40	12	SR(2)
Siren	1960	1,425	221	38	12½ .	DE(2)

Corporation of Trinity House (Continued)

Name	Built	Tons	Length	Breadth	Speed	Engines
Stella	1961	1,425	221	38	12½	DE(2)
Vestal	1947	1,918	268	40	12	SR(2)
Winston Churchill	1963	1,451	222	38	12½	DE(2)
Pilot Tenders:						
Pathfinder	1954	678	175	30	10	M(2)
Patricia	1938	1,073	232	36	10	M(2)
Pelorus	1948	443	153	28	· 9	M(2)
Penlee	1948	443	153	28	9	M(2)
Preceder	1961	335	139	24	10	M(2)

PORT OF LONDON AUTHORITY

London

FUNNEL: Yellow.
HULL: Black.

Name	Built	Tons	Length	Breadth	Speed	Engines
Salvage and Buoy Vessels:						
Broadness ✓	1965	235	114	28	8	DE(2)(A)
Crossness	1969	268	127	28	9	M(2)(A)
Hookness	1969	268	127	28	9½	M(2)(A)
Stoneness ✓	1965	233	114	28	9	DE(2)(A)
Yantlet ✓	1955	471	154	32	9½	M

See also Tugs and Harbour Works & Dredging Craft

BRITISH TRANSPORT DOCKS BOARD

Hull & Southampton

FUNNEL: Blue with white "bollard" device.
HULL: Black.

Name	Built	Tons	Length	Breadth	Speed	Engines
Buoy Vessel:						
Humber Guardian	1967	618	170	33	12½	M(2)(A)

OIL RIG SERVICING, SAFETY AND SUPPLY VESSELS AND RESEARCH VESSELS

BREYDON MARINE LTD

Lowestoft

FUNNEL: Red.
HULL: Black with red boot-topping.

Name	Built	Tons	Length	Breadth	Speed	Engines
Oil Rig Safety Vessel:						
Breydon Widgeon ex Boston Widgeon-73	1961	165	94	22	9	M

COSAG MARINE SERVICES LTD

London

FUNNEL: Blue.
HULL: Black with red boot-topping.

Name	Built	Tons	Length	Breadth	Speed	Engines
Research Vessel:						
Max Reimann	1951	264	129	24	9	M
Sperus ex Hesperus-74	1939	922	211	36	12	M(2)
Tikker ex Sheila Homan-71, Rostock-70	1951	255	129	24	9	M

DECCA NAVIGATOR CO LTD

London

FUNNEL: Blue with "DS" monogram on white bordered blue diamond and black top.
HULL: Black with white line and red boot-topping.

Name	Built	Tons	Length	Breadth	Speed	Engines
Research Vessel:						
Decca Engineer ex Lady Claudine-73	1966	620	158	37	13	M(2)(A)
Decca Scanner ex Warwick Bay-73	1968	1,018	170	36	12½	M(A)
Decca Pilot ex Patrol-72	1961	335	139	24	11	M
Decca Recorder ex Clearwater-73	1970	299	127	28	12	M(2)
Decca Surveyor ex Britonnia-72	1963	600	158	33	13	M

DUNEDALE LTD

Douglas, I.O.M.

FUNNEL: Red with yellow Manx emblem.
HULL: Black with red boot-topping.

Name	Built	Tons	Length	Breadth	Speed	Engines
Tender/Oil Rig Safety Vessel:						
Lady Cora ex Boston Valetta-73, Acadia Fin-Fare-68, Boston Valetta-61	1956	239	111	24	10	M

GARDLINE SHIPPING LTD

Lowestoft

FUNNEL: Yellow with black letter "G" on white diamond on broad red band.
HULL: Black with red boot-topping.

Name	Built	Tons	Length	Breadth	Speed	Engines
Research Vessels:						
Charterer	1955	477	187	29	11	M(A)
ex Tananger-73						
Endurer	1954	431	174	29	10½	M(A)
Observer	1943	306	133	23	10	M(A)
ex Inspector-72,						
Hornöy-70,						
Grane, Adolf						
von Trotha						
Profiler	1955	995	207	37	12	SR(A)
ex lerne-73						
Researcher	1950	433	144	26	12	M(A)
ex Ingöy-71						
Tracker	1954	431	174	29	11	M(A)
ex Ryfylke-73						

HARRISON'S (CLYDE) LTD

Glasgow

FUNNEL: Red with black top and red letter "H" on three blue vertical lines on white shield.
HULL: Blue with red boot-topping.

Name	Built	Tons	Length	Breadth	Speed	Engines
Oil Rig Supply/Service Vessels:						
Stirling Brig	1974	700			14	M(2)(A)
Stirling Eagle	1974	700			14	M(2)(A)
Stirling Rock	1974	700			14	M(A)(2)
Stirling Oak	1974	700			14	M(A)(2)

OIL VENTURER, Ocean Inchcape Ltd *J. Clarkson*

INTERNATIONAL OFFSHORE SERVICES LTD
(Tidewater Marine Service Inc.)

London

FUNNEL: Yellow with black top and blue anchor device.
HULL: Black with red boot-topping.

Name	Built	Tons	Length	Breadth	Speed	Engines
Oil Rig Supply/Service Vessels:						
Lady Claudine	1966	620	158	37	13	M(2)(A)
Lady Delia	1966	773	170	38	13	M(2)(A)
Lady Fiona	1966	773	170	38	13	M(2)(A)
Lady Sarah	1972	987	190	43	14	M(2)(A)
New (2)	1974/75					M(2)(A)

NATURAL ENVIRONMENT RESEARCH COUNCIL

London

FUNNEL: Yellow with black top.
HULL: Black with white line and red boot-topping.

Name	Built	Tons	Length	Breadth	Speed	Engines
Research Vessels:						
Edward Forbes ex Offshore Delight-72, Ross Delight-68	1964	183	89	23	11	M
John Murray ex Noblesse-66	1963	441	122	26	11	M

Other Vessels employed in Antarctica

OCEAN INCHCAPE LTD

London

FUNNEL: Red with black top and black letters "OIL" on white band.
HULL: Grey with red boot-topping.

Name	Built	Tons	Length	Breadth	Speed	Engines
Oil Rig Towing/Servicing/Supply Vessels:						
Oil Discoverer	1973	855	196	43	$15\frac{1}{4}$	M(2)

Ocean Inchcape Ltd (Continued)

Name	Built	Tons	Length	Breadth	Speed	Engines
Oil Driller	1973	852	196	43	$15\frac{3}{4}$	M(2)
Oil Explorer	1972	743	188	42	$14\frac{1}{4}$	M(2)
Oil Mariner	1973	852	195	43	$15\frac{3}{4}$	M(2)
Oil Producer	1972	743	188	43	$14\frac{1}{4}$	M(2)
Oil Prospector	1972	743	188	43	$14\frac{1}{4}$	M(2)
Oil Supplier	1972	743	188	43	$14\frac{1}{4}$	M(2)
Oil Venturer	1973	853	195	43	$15\frac{1}{4}$	M(2)
New (2)	1975					M(2)
Production Testing Vessel:						
Oil Dragon*	1943	693	206	35	$12\frac{1}{2}$	M(2)(A)
ex Duchess of Holland-73, Viper, LSM 250						
Seismic Survey Vessel:						
Oil Hunter	1963	791	190	32	15	M
ex Lofottral I-74						

* *Converted 1973, on long term charter to FLOPETROL*

OFFSHORE MARINE LTD

London

FUNNEL: Yellow with black top and red letters "O" above "M".
HULL: Grey with red boot-topping.

Name	Built	Tons	Length	Breadth	Speed	Engines
Oil Rig Service/Supply Vessels:						
Arctic Shore	1968	677	177	38	12	M(2)(A)
Atlantic Shore	1968	499	167	36	$12\frac{1}{2}$	M(2)(A)
Bay Shore	1971	694	184	38	$13\frac{3}{4}$	M(2)(A)
Cape Shore	1970	694	184	38	$14\frac{1}{2}$	M(2)(A)
Channel Shore	1972	695	183	38	$14\frac{1}{4}$	M(2)(A)
Cromarty Shore	1973	900	195	42	$14\frac{1}{2}$	M(2)(A)
Dogger Shore	1973	898	196	43	$13\frac{1}{2}$	M(2)(A)
Essex Shore	1967	499	167	36	13	M(2)(A)
Fastnet Shore	1974	900	195	42	$14\frac{1}{2}$	M(2)(A)
Forties Shore	1974	900	195	42	$14\frac{1}{2}$	M(2)(A)
Island Shore	1970	694	184	38	$13\frac{3}{4}$	M(2)(A)

Offshore Marine Ltd (Continued)

Name	Built	Tons	Length	Breadth	Speed	Engines
Kent Shore	1967	664	177	38	12	M(2)(A)
Lundy Shore	1973	900	195	42	14½	M(2)(A)
Norfolk Shore	1967	499	159	34	12¾	M(2)(A)
North Shore	1965	677	165	38	12	M(2)(A)
Nova Shore	1969	677	177	38	12	M(2)(A)
Ocean Shore	1972	695	183	38	14½	M(2)(A)
Orkney Shore	1973	699	176	38	14½	M(2)(A)
Pacific Shore	1969	678	177	38	12½	M(2)(A)
Petrel Shore	1970	412	137	33	12	M(2)(A)
Polar Shore	1971	700	185	39	14	M(2)(A)
Shetland Shore	1973	699	176	38	14½	M(2)(A)
Strait Shore	1970	498	167	36	13½	M(2)(A)
Suffolk Shore	1967	663	172	38	12	M(2)(A)
Tropic Shore	1969	499	167	36	12½	M(2)(A)
Viking Shore	1973	900	195	42	14½	M(2)(A)
Canadian Offshore Marine Ltd:						
Breton Shore	1973	699	185	39	13¾	M(2)(A)
Scotian Shore	1973	699	185	39	13¾	M(2)(A)
Offshore Marine Ltd:						
Bass Shore	1973	730	185	39	14	M(2)(A)
Cook Shore	1969	708	177	38	12½	M(2)(A)

OFFSHORE OIL RIG SERVICES LTD

Jersey, C.I.

FUNNEL: Black with black diamond on broad red band.
HULL: Black with red boot-topping.

Name	Built	Tons	Length	Breadth	Speed	Engines
Oil Rig Safety Vessel:						
Young Elizabeth	1953	115	88	21	9	M

PLESSEY LTD

London

FUNNEL: None.
HULL: Blue with red boot-topping.

Name	Built	Tons	Length	Breadth	Speed	Engines
Research Vessel:						
Sono ex LCU-69	1945	167	110	32	7	M(3)

MRS L. A. RODGER
(JR Marine Ltd)

London

FUNNEL: Yellow with black top.
HULL: White with black boot-topping.

Name	Built	Tons	Length	Breadth	Speed	Engines
Research Vessel:						
Lady of Essex ex Steigen-68	1953	283	128	24	11	M(A)

SAFETYSHIPS LTD
(Boston Group Holdings Ltd & The John Wood Group (Aberdeen) Ltd)

Aberdeen

FUNNEL: Red with black top.
HULL: Black with white line and red boot-topping.

Name	Built	Tons	Length	Breadth	Speed	Engines
Oil Rig Safety Ships:						
Bannockburn ex Sutton- Queen-71	1957	178	103	22	11	M

Safetyships Ltd (Continued)

Name	Built	Tons	Length	Breadth	Speed	Engines
Carbisdale ex Boston Trident-72, John O'Heugh- 63	1957	182	102	22	11	M
Dunnichen ex Boston Caravelle-73, Diadem-63	1954	166	103	22	10	M
Kilsyth ex Penzance Pegasus-73, Boston Pegasus-71	1954	166	103	22	10	M
Ocean Trust	1957	113	91	21	9	M
Otterburn ex Boston Vulcan-72, St. Hilda-63	1955	182	102	22	10½	M
Sheriffmuir	1952	180	102	22	10	M

SEAFORTH MARITIME LTD

Aberdeen

FUNNEL: Yellow with black top and company device in red.
HULL:

Name	Built	Tons	Length	Breadth	Speed	Engines
Oil Rig Supply/Service Vessels:						
Seaforth Challenger	1973	1,000	180	39	13	M(2)
Seaforth Chieftain	1973	776	189	40	13	M(2)
Seaforth Hero	1973	1,000	180	39	13	M(2)
Seaforth Prince	1973	733	189	40	13	M(2)
New (4)	1974/75	1,000dw			13½	M(2)
Seaforth Champion	1974	770				
Seaforth Saga						
Seaforth Victor	1974	750				
Seaforth Viking						

SEA SERVICES SHIPPING CO LTD

Folkestone

FUNNEL : Blue with black top.
HULL : Various colours.

Name	Built	Tons	Length	Breadth	Speed	Engines
Oil Rig Supply/Service Vessels:						
Aberdeen Blazer ex Lady Alison-74	1965	854	188	38	12½	M(2)(A)
Border Blazer ex South Shore-73	1965	451	149	35	11	M(2)(A)
Galway Blazer ex Namsos-69	1954	499	146	26	11	M(A)
Highland Blazer ex Ranen-68	1958	487	162	28	11	M(A)
Lowland Blazer ex Lady Brigid-74	1966	677	158	38	12½	M(2)(A)
New	1974	750dw				M(2)(A)

SPURN SHIPPING CO LTD

Grimsby

FUNNEL : Blue with black and white lighthouse on black rock.
HULL :

Name	Built	Tons	Length	Breadth	Speed	Engines
Oil Rig Supply/Service Vessel:						
Spurn Haven ex Lady Edwina-70	1966	247	105	26	12	M(2)

THERIOT OFFSHORE INTERNATIONAL LTD

Great Yarmouth & Leith

FUNNEL: White with company device in red and blue.
HULL: Black.

Name	Built	Tons	Length	Breadth	Speed	Engines
Oil Rig Towing/Servicing/Supply Vessels:						
Theriot Offshore I	1974	1,000dw			14	M(2)
Theriot Offshore II	1974	1,000dw			14	M(2)
New(10)	1975/76	1,000dw			14	

VICKERS OCEANICS LTD

Barrow

FUNNEL: Yellow with company symbol in blue.
HULL: Blue with red boot-topping.

Name	Built	Tons	Length	Breadth	Speed	Engines
Research and Diving Vessels:						
Vickers Venture ex Relko-68	1963	320	122	26	12	M
Vickers Viking ex Dortmund-74, Danasbank-70, Hamburg-67	1965	1,599	240	45	15	M
Vickers Viscount ex Meath-74	1960	1,588	289	45	13	M
Vickers Voyager ex Fairtry II-72	1959	3,004	275	48	13	DE

WIMPEY (MARINE) LTD

London

FUNNEL: Brown with black top.
HULL: Black with red boot-topping.

Name	Built	Tons	Length	Breadth	Speed	Engines
Oil Rig Supply/Service Vessels:						
Wimbrown One	1965	697	162	37	13	M(2)
Wimbrown Two	1965	700	162	37	13	M(2)
Wimbrown Three	1966	696	162	37	13	M(2)
Wimpey Seadog	1973	907	194	42	13½	M(2)
Wimpey Sealion	1973	907	194	42	13½	M(2)
New (3)	1974/75	1,000dw			14	M(2)
Drilling Vessel:						
Wimpey Sealab ex Elizabeth Bowater-72	1958	3,914	325	50	12	M

ZAPATA OFFSHORE SERVICES LTD

London

FUNNEL: White with black trident device.
HULL: Dark grey with green boot-topping.

Name	Built	Tons	Length	Breadth	Speed	Engines
Oil Rig Supply/Service Vessels.						
Imperial Service	1971	689	184	39	16	M(2)(A)
Majestic Service	1972	688	185	39	16½	M(2)(A)
Monarch Service	1972	692	185	39	16	M(2)(A)
Paramount Service	1971	692	185	39	16	M(2)(A)

HARBOUR WORKS AND DREDGING CRAFT

ARDROSSAN HARBOUR CO LTD

Ardrossan

FUNNEL: Black with houseflag on broad white band.
HULL: Black with white line and red boot-topping.

Name	Built	Tons	Length	Breadth	Speed	Engines
Bucket Dredger:						
Sir William H. Raeburn	1928	253	128	27	7½	S R(2)(A)

See also Tugs

BLYTH HARBOUR COMMISSIONERS

Blyth

FUNNEL: Cream with black top.
HULL: Black with white line.

Name	Built	Tons	Length	Breadth	Speed	Engines
Grab Hopper Dredger:						
Cresswell	1959	374	136	30	10	M(A)
Trailing Suction Dredger:						
Crofton	1963	1,062	195	42	12	DE(2)(A)

See also Tugs

PORT OF BOSTON AUTHORITY

Boston, Lincs.

FUNNEL: White with black top.
HULL: Black with red boot-topping.

Name	Built	Tons	Length	Breadth	Speed	Engines
Grab Hopper Dredger:						
Jean Ingelow	1950	149	104	25	7½	M(A)

See also Tugs

PORT OF BRISTOL AUTHORITY

Bristol

FUNNEL: Black with broad white band with red rectangles thereon.
HULL: Black with dark grey topsides.

Name	Built	Tons	Length	Breadth	Speed	Engines
Grab Hopper Dredger:						
Clifton	1968	1,150	202	44	10½	M(2)(A)
Suction Hopper Dredger:						
S. D. Severn	1966	1,287	212	44	10	M(2)(A)
Hopper Barges:						
Avon	1956	542	175	30	9½	M(2)(A)
Frome	1956	542	175	30	9½	M(2)(A)
Kingroad	1953	1,046	199	39	9½	M(2)(A)

BRITISH TRANSPORT DOCKS BOARD

London

FUNNEL: Blue with white "bollard" device.
HULL: Black.

Name	Built	Tons	Length	Breadth	Speed	Engines
Grab Hopper Dredgers:						

British Transport Docks Board (Continued)

Name	Built	Tons	Length	Breadth	Speed	Engines
Aberavon	1969	2,156	251	50	10	M(A)
Breckland	1960	418	133	33	9½	M(A)
Burcom Sand	1954	678	170	34	9½	M(A)
Calatria	1961	1,034	201	39	10	M(A)
Cave Sand	1968	1,080	206	41	10½	M(A)
Cherry Sand	1968	1,080	206	40	10½	M(A)
Ely	1961	1,430	228	45	9¾	M(A)
Goole Bight	1958	325	119	29	9	M(A)
Grassendale	1954	677	165	34	9	M(A)
Haile Sand	1963	869	157	34	9½	M(A)
Hebble Sand	1963	869	157	34	9½	M(A)
Kenfig	1954	677	165	34	9	M(A)
Lake Lothing	1955	659	165	34	9	M(A)
Ogmore	1967	609	150	35	10	M(A)
Oyster Sand	1966	609	150	35	10	M(A)
Redcliffe Sand	1964	1,424	214	45	11	M(A)
Rhymney	1960	710	165	35	9	M(A)
Trinity Sand	1961	1,252	212	45	9½	M(A)
Trailing Suction Hopper Dredgers:						
Baglan	1966	1,889	250	48	12	DE(A)
Bleasdale	1962	1,029	193	40	10½	DE(A)
Clee Ness	1962	1,436	223	45	10	M(A)
Lavernock	1967	1,864	250	48	12	DE(A)
Skitter Ness	1964	1,577	230	45	11	DE(A)

See also Tugs

THE CATTEWATER HARBOUR COMMISSIONERS

Plymouth

FUNNEL: Red with black top and white letters "CHC".
HULL: Black with red boot-topping.

Name	Built	Tons	Length	Breadth	Speed	Engines
Grab Hopper Dredger:						
Plymsand ex Mersey No. 14-71	1949	459	145	32	10	DE(A)
Hopper Barge:						
Liarsand ex W. 34-71	1947	273	135	22	8	M(A)

CLYDE PORT AUTHORITY

Glasgow

FUNNEL: Yellow with or without black top.
HULL: Blue with red boot-topping.

Name	Built	Tons	Length	Breadth	Speed	Engines
Bucket Dredger:						
Blythswood	1963	786	210	43	9	M(2)(A)
Grab Hopper Dredger:						
Lennox II	1954	795	192	38	10½	SR(2)(A)
Hopper Barges:						
Hopper No. 25	1954	941	210	37	10½	SR(2)(A)
Hopper No. 26	1954	941	210	37	10½	SR(2)(A)
Hopper No. 27	1962	981	208	37	11	M(2)(A)
Hopper No. 28	1963	981	208	37	11	M(2)(A)

CONOLEY & CO LTD

Falmouth

FUNNEL: Red with black top.
HULL: Black.

Name	Built	Tons	Length	Breadth	Speed	Engines
Grab Hopper Dredger:						
Rosslyn	1912	702	196	41	7½	SR(A)

D. COOK LTD

Hull

FUNNEL: Red with black top.
HULL: Black with red boot-topping.

Name	Built	Tons	Length	Breadth	Speed	Engines
Grab Hopper Dredger:						
Foremost 50	1937	380	142	30	8½	SR(A)

COSTAIN BLANKEVOORT (UK) DREDGING CO LTD

London

FUNNEL: Blue with blue letter "C" on white panel.
HULL: Grey or blue with black boot-topping.

Name	Built	Tons	Length	Breadth	Speed	Engines
Trailing Suction Hopper Dredgers:						
Delta Bay	1971	7,986	410	65	13½	M(2)
Tees Bay	1966	2,941	310	54	12	M(2)(A)
ex Cap d'Antifer-72, Tees Bay-70						
Hopper Barges:						
Thames Bay	1967	605	177	31	8	M(2)(A)
Tyne Bay	1967	606	177	31	8	M(2)(A)
Sand Dredger and Carrier:						
Eric Cooper	1965	553	157	34	9	M(A)

DEPARTMENT OF THE ENVIRONMENT

Portsmouth, Plymouth, etc

FUNNEL: Black with black letter "W" on white diamond.
HULL: Black with grey topsides.

Name	Built	Tons	Length	Breadth	Speed	Engines
Grab Hopper Dredgers:						
St. Giles (W.6)	1951	619			9	SR(2)(A)
St. Martin (W.8)	1951	389			8½	SR(2)(A)
Servitor (W.9)	1935	572			9	SR(2)(A)

DOVER HARBOUR BOARD

Dover

FUNNEL: Black with white letters "DH" on broad red band between narrow
white bands.
HULL: Black with white line and red boot-topping.

Name	Built	Tons	Length	Breadth	Speed	Engines
Grab Hopper Dredger:						
Admiral Day	1971	350	134	31	8½	M(2)(A)

See also Tugs

DREDGING & CONSTRUCTION CO LTD

King's Lynn

FUNNEL: Black with houseflag panel on broad white band between narrow
red bands.
HULL: Grey with black boot-topping or black with red boot-topping.

Name	Built	Tons	Length	Breadth	Speed	Engines
Trailing Suction Hopper Dredger:						
Geopotes X	1970	10.703	446	71	17	M(2)(A)
Hopper Barge:						
Red Nab	1960	717	180	36	9	M(A)
Dredging & Construction Co Ltd/ Nash Dredging & Reclamation Co Ltd:						
A. D. Geopotes I	1972	4,000	315	55	13	M(2)(A)

FORTH PORTS AUTHORITY

Leith

FUNNEL: Black.
HULL: Black with white line and red boot-topping.

Name	Built	Tons	Length	Breadth	Speed	Engines
Trailing Suction Hopper Dredger:						
Abbotsgrange	1967	1,864	250	48	12	DE(2)(A)

See also Tugs

FOWEY HARBOUR COMMISSIONERS

Fowey

FUNNEL: Yellow with black top.
HULL: Grey with red boot-topping.

Name	Built	Tons	Length	Breadth	Speed	Engines
Grab Hopper Dredger:						
Lantic Bay	1958	148	112	24	7½	M(A)

IPSWICH PORT AUTHORITY

Ipswich

FUNNEL: Brown with black top.
HULL: Black.

Name	Built	Tons	Length	Breadth	Speed	Engines
Grab Hopper Dredger:						
Samual Armstrong	1956	364	136	30	9	M(A)

ISLE OF MAN HARBOUR BOARD

Douglas, I.O.M.

FUNNEL: Red with black top.
HULL: Black.

Name	Built	Tons	Length	Breadth	Speed	Engines
Grab Hopper Dredger:						
Mannin	1972	173	104	26	8½	M(A)

PORT OF LONDON AUTHORITY

London

FUNNEL: Yellow.
HULL: Black.

Name	Built	Tons	Length	Breadth	Speed	Engines
Hopper Barges:						
Asa Binns ✓	1964	847	205	35	8	M(2)(A) SCH
Cyril Kirkpatrick ✓	1964	847	205	35	8	M(2)(A) SCH

See also Tugs

MANCHESTER SHIP CANAL CO LTD

Manchester

FUNNEL: Black with two white bands.
HULL: Black.

Name	Built	Tons	Length	Breadth	Speed	Engines
Bucket Dredger:						
Gowy	1924	415	160	36	7	SR(A)

Name	Built	Tons	Length	Breadth	Speed	Engines
Grab Hopper Dredgers:						
Grab Hopper No. 1	1949	479	150	32	8	M(A)
Grab Hopper No. 2	1959	129	103	25	8	M(2)(A)

See also Tugs

MERSEY DOCKS & HARBOUR COMPANY

Liverpool

FUNNEL: Yellow with black top.
HULL: Dark grey with red boot-topping.

Name	Built	Tons	Length	Breadth	Speed	Engines
Grab Hopper Dredgers:						
Mersey Compass	1961	2,083	275	48	12	DE(2)(A)
Mersey No. 40	1957	1,968	263	48	11½	M(2)(A)
Mersey No. 41	1957	1,364	238	41	11	M(2)(A)

See also Pilot Lighthouse & Buoy Tenders

NASH DREDGING & RECLAMATION CO LTD

Guildford

FUNNEL: White with white over red diamond on blue panel and blue top.
HULL: Dark blue with red boot-topping.

Name	Built	Tons	Length	Breadth	Speed	Engines
Trailing Suction Hopper Dredger:						
Van Hattum en Blankevoort 20	1968	4,821	343	59	12½	M(2)(A)

POOLE HARBOUR COMMISSIONERS

Poole

FUNNEL: None.
HULL: Black with red topsides.

Name	Built	Tons	Length	Breadth	Speed	Engines
Grab Hopper Dredger:						
C. H. Horn	1968	159	85	29	6½	M(A)

PORT OF PRESTON AUTHORITY

Preston

FUNNEL: Black with Corporation armorial shield in pale blue and white.
HULL: Black.

Name	Built	Tons	Length	Breadth	Speed	Engines
Suction Hopper Dredgers:						
Robert Weir	1957	1,030	199	42	9	SR(A)
Savick	1949	618	173	32	8½	SR(A)

See also Tugs

BOROUGH OF RAMSGATE

Ramsgate

FUNNEL: Red with black top.
HULL: Grey with red boot-topping.

Name	Built	Tons	Length	Breadth	Speed	Engines
Grab Hopper Dredger:						
Ramsgate	1962	168	102	26	8	M(A)

SCARBOROUGH CORPORATION

Scarborough

FUNNEL: Yellow.
HULL: Black with red boot-topping.

Name	Built	Tons	Length	Breadth	Speed	Engines
Grab Hopper Dredger:						
Skarthi	1952	112	84	23	7	M(A)

SEAHAM HARBOUR DOCK CO LTD

Seaham

FUNNEL: Black with broad red band.
HULL: Black with red boot-topping.

Name	Built	Tons	Length	Breadth	Speed	Engines
Grab Hopper Dredger:						
Wynyard ex Ramsgate-62	1936	220	109	27	7½	SR(A)

See also Tugs

SHOREHAM PORT AUTHORITY

Shoreham

FUNNEL: Black.
HULL: Black.

Name	Built	Tons	Length	Breadth	Speed	Engines
Bucket Dredger:						
Adur MEDWAY.SHI.	1954	199	148	25	6	SR(A)

See also Tugs

PORT OF SUNDERLAND AUTHORITY

Sunderland

FUNNEL: Yellow with black top and black sextant.
HULL: Black with white line and red boot-topping.

Name	Built	Tons	Length	Breadth	Speed	Engines
Hopper Barges:						
Wear Hopper No. 3	1959	414	150	30	8½	M(A)
Wear Hopper No. 4	1959	414	150	30	8½	M(A)

See also Tugs

TAYLOR WOODROW INTERNATIONAL LTD

London

FUNNEL: Black with four red "men" on broad white band.
HULL: Black with red boot-topping.

Name	Built	Tons	Length	Breadth	Speed	Engines
Trailing Suction Hopper Dredger:						
Transmundum II	1969	2,961	312	53	10	M(2)(A)

TEES & HARTLEPOOLS PORT AUTHORITY

Middlesbrough

FUNNEL: Turquoise with orange or gold company device and black top.
HULL: Black with red boot-topping.

Name	Built	Tons	Length	Breadth	Speed	Engines
Suction Hopper Dredger:						
T.C.C. Dredger No. I	1951	1,206	220	41	9	SR(2)(A)

Name	Built	Tons	Length	Breadth	Speed	Engines
Hopper Dredgers:						
Cleveland County	1973	656	158	40	9	M(2)(A)
Heortnesse	1959	604	156	43	9	M(2)(A)
Seal Sands	1973	656	158	41	10	M(2)(A)

PORT OF TYNE AUTHORITY

Newcastle

FUNNEL: Yellow with black top, some with numbers, in black.
HULL: Black with red boot-topping.

Name	Built	Tons	Length	Breadth	Speed	Engines
Grab Hopper Dredger:						
Hedwin	1969	666	157	39	8	M(A)
Hopper Barges:						
T.I.C. No. 26	1956	477	150	32	9	M(A)
T.I.C. No. 27	1956	477	150	32	9	M(A)

UML LTD
(Unilever Ltd)

Bebington, Cheshire

FUNNEL: Yellow with green top.
HULL: Green.

Name	Built	Tons	Length	Breadth	Speed	Engines
Grab Hopper Dredger:						
Sand Swallow II	1947	222	112	24	9	M(A)

WESTMINSTER DREDGING CO LTD
(Westminster Dredging Group Ltd)

London

FUNNEL: Black with diagonal yellow over blue panel or white with black top and diagonal yellow over blue panel on superstructure.
HULL: Black or grey with black or red boot-topping.

Name	Built	Tons	Length	Breadth	Speed	Engines
Trailing Suction Hopper Dredgers:						
Prins der Nederlanden	1968	10,482	468	72	16	M(2)(A)
The Solent ex H.A.M. 303	1958	2,105	300	45	12	M(2)(A)
W.D. Fairway	1941	1,299	227	39	11	M(2)(A)
W.D. Gateway	1969	8,168	423	64	16	M(2)(A)
W.D. Hilbre	1967	1,112	214	39	13	M(2)(A)
W.D. Hoyle	1967	1,223	233	39	11	M(2)(A)
W.D. Mersey	1960	2,851	301	53	11	M(2)(A)
W.D. Seaway	1963	4,712	360	60	12	M(2)(A)
W.D. Seven Seas Beaver	1959	2,034	291	44	12	M(2)(A)
Mackenzie ex W. D. Thames -74, Batavus-65	1939	1,887	258	43	11	M(2)(A)
W.D. Tideway	1966	4,030	332	55	12	M(2)(A)
W.D. Waterway ex W.D. 52-62, Marga	1941	1,424	249	39	10½	M(2)(A)
Suction Hopper Dredger:						
Merstone ex James No. .96-67, Kalberdans-50	1939	413	168	28	8½	M(A)
Grab Hopper Dredger:						
W.D. Cressington ex Cressington	1962	1,431	213	46	12	M(A)
Hopper Barges:						
Barrow Deep	1926	911	190	39	7	M(2)(A) SCH
Black Deep	1925	914	190	39	7	M(2)(A) SCH
Foremost 102	1940	871	194	33	8½	M(A)
James No. 95 ex Witt Kliff-50	1939	433	168	28	8½	M(A)
Lune Deep	1936	895	190	40	7	M(2)(A)

Sold 10.81

Westminster Dredging Co Ltd (Continued)

Name	Built	Tons	Length	Breadth	Speed	Engines
South Deep	1936	917	197	40	7	M(2)(A)
W.D. 54*	1937	1,105	230	38	10	SR(2)(A)
W.D. Avon	1974				10	M(A)
W.D. Clyde	1963	1,078	214	38	10	M(A)
W.D. Severn	1974				10	M(A)
W.D. Itchen	1970	1,193	230	43	9½	M(A)
W.D. Test	1970	1,193	230	43	9½	M(A)
launched as						
Foremost Test						
W.D. Tyne	1963	1,079	214	38	11	M(A)
Bunkering Tanker:						
James No. 81	1937	183	101	26	9	M(A)

* Laid up. See also Tugs and Westminster Gravels Ltd

IRISH REPUBLIC

COMMISSIONERS OF PUBLIC WORKS IN IRELAND
Dublin
FUNNEL: Black.
HULL: Black.

Name	Built	Tons	Length	Breadth	Speed	Engines
Bucket Hopper Dredger:						
Sisyphus	1905	284	119	26	7	SR

CORK HARBOUR COMMISSIONERS
Cork
FUNNEL: White with black top.
HULL: Black.

Name	Built	Tons	Length	Breadth	Speed	Engines
Grab Hopper Dredgers:						
Grabwell	1935	251	115	28	8½	SR(A)
Loughmahon II	1964	250	129	28	8½	M(A)
Ringacoltig	1973	400	134	33	9	M(A)

See also Tugs

LIMERICK HARBOUR COMMISSIONERS

Limerick

FUNNEL:
HULL:

Name	Built	Tons	Length	Breadth	Speed	Engines
Grab and Suction Dredger:						
Curraghgour II	1959	457	143	33	8	M(A)

NITRIGIN EIREANN TEORANTA

Arklow

FUNNEL: Green with black top and white letters "NET".
HULL: Grey.

Name	Built	Tons	Length	Breadth	Speed	Engines
Suction Hopper Dredger						
Tredagh ex Bela-71, Tredagh-70	1958	196	116	22	9	M(A)

TUGS

ABERDEEN HARBOUR BOARD

Aberdeen

FUNNEL: Black with letters "AHB" on broad yellow band between narrow red bands.
HULL: Black with white line and red boot-topping.
AREA OF OPERATION: Aberdeen and Invergordon.

Name	Built	Tons Gross	Horse Power	Engines
Sea Griffon	1962	117	800(B)	M
Sea Trojan	1962	117	800(B)	M

ALEXANDRA TOWING CO LTD

Liverpool

FUNNEL: Yellow with black top separated by broad white band over narrow black band.
HULL: Black with yellow top line and red boot-topping.
AREA OF OPERATION: Liverpool and River Mersey; Southampton and the Solent; Swansea, Port Talbot and the Bristol Channel; Continental, UK & Irish coastal towage.

Name	Built	Tons Gross	Horse Power	Engines
Albert	1972	272	2,400(B)	M
Alexandra	1963	161	940(B)	M
Alfred	1972	272	2,400(B)	M
Brockenhurst	1964	173	1,200(B)	M
Brocklebank	1965	172	1,200(B)	M
Crosby	1972	272	2,400(B)	M/K/FF
Egerton	1965	172	1,200(B)	M
Gower	1961	152	960(B)	M
Herculaneum	1962	161	940(B)	M/K
Langton	1964	172	1,200(B)	M
Margam	1970	278	2,190(B)	M/K/FF
Mumbles	1969	291	2,190(B)	M/K
Nelson	1966	173	1,200(B)	M
North Isle	1959	200	1,350(B)	M
North Loch	1959	200	1,350(B)	M
Romsey	1964	173	1,200(B)	M
Talbot	1961	153	960(B)	M
Trafalgar	1966	173	1,200(B)	M
Ventnor	1965	173	1,200(B)	M
Victoria	1972	272	2,400(B)	M
J. H. Lamey Ltd:				
Coburg ex Alfred Lamey-70	1967	219	1,700(B)	M
Hornby ex J. H. Lamey-70	1964	216	1,350(B)	M
Huskisson ex James Lamey-70	1968	219	1,350(B)	M
Salthouse ex B. C. Lamey-70	1966	225	1,380(B)	M
Wapping ex William Lamey-70	1959	166	1,000(B)	M
Liverpool Screw Towing Co Ltd:				
Canada ex Pea Cock-70	1960	159	1,080(B)	M
Collingwood ex Heath Cock-70	1958	193	1,170(B)	M
Formby ex Weather Cock-70	1960	159	1,080(B)	M
Gladstone ex Flying Cock-70	1960	159	1,080(B)	M
Morpeth	1958	192	1,170(B)	M

Top: W. D. MERSEY, Westminster Dredging Co Ltd *F. R. Sherlock*
Centre: ALFRED, Alexandra Towing Co Ltd *J. K. Byass*
Bottom: ARDNEIL, Ardrossan Harbour Co Ltd *J. Clarkson*

ARC MARINE LTD
(Amey Roadstone Corp Ltd)
(Gold Fields Group)

Southampton

FUNNEL: Blue with white band.
HULL: Black with red boot-topping.
AREA OF OPERATION: Rivers Stour and Orwell.

Name	Built	Tons Gross	Horse Power	Engines
Arco Deben ex Pen Deben-73	1928	45	250(B)	M rbt fm SR

See also Coastal Ships

ARDROSSAN HARBOUR CO LTD

Ardrossan

FUNNEL: Black with broad white band.
HULL: Black with white line and red boot-topping.
AREA OF OPERATION: Ardossan.

Name	Built	Tons Gross	Horse Power	Engines
Ardneil ex Cruiser-69	1953	300	1,350(B)	M rbt fm SR

See also Harbour Works and Dredging Craft

F. A. ASHMEAD & SONS LTD

Avonmouth

FUNNEL: Black with red letter "A" on broad white band between narrow red bands.
HULL: Grey with red boot-topping.
AREA OF OPERATION: Bristol, Avonmouth and Bristol Channel (Lighterage).

Name	Built	Tons Gross	Horse Power	Engines
Peter Leigh ex John King-70	1936	49	300(B)	M

F. A. Ashmead & Sons Ltd (Continued)

Name	Built	Tons Gross	Horse Power	Engines
Robert A. ex Volunteer-59	1934	32	200(B)	M
Thelm Leigh ex Resolute-70	1897	64	360(B)	M rbt fm SR

Also the smaller tugs Judith A. and Hubert A.

See also Coastal Ships

ASSOCIATED PORTLAND CEMENT MANUFACTURERS LTD

London

FUNNEL: Black with white band bordered by blue and yellow bands.
HULL: Black with two white lines and red boot-topping.
AREA OF OPERATION: River Thames and Medway (Company's Lighterage).

Name	Built	Tons Gross	Horse Power	Engines
Cemenco	1948	116	720(B)	M
Cullamix	1938	96	650(B)	M
Imperno ex Benbow-60, Temeritie	1935	38	200(B)	M
Sandtex ex Silverdial-70	1950	92	605(B)	M

A. M. BARKER

Gravesend

FUNNEL: Black with white band.
HULL: Blue or grey.
AREA OF OPERATION: Contract Work, River Thames and Towage S.E. Coast.

e	Built	Tons Gross	Horse Power	Engines
Albatross				
Cormorant ex Maud-73	1956		200(B)	M

BELFAST HARBOUR COMMISSIONERS

Belfast

FUNNEL: Yellow with black top.
HULL: Black with red boot-topping.
AREA OF OPERATION: Belfast and Belfast Lough.

Name	Built	Tons Gross	Horse Power	Engines
Ada Dorothy	1971	54	337(B)	M
David Andrews	1971	54	337(B)	M

BLYTH HARBOUR COMMISSIONERS

Blyth

FUNNEL: Cream with black top.
HULL: Black with white line.
AREA OF OPERATION: Blyth.

Name	Built	Tons Gross	Horse Power	Engines
Horton	1968	31	240(B)	M/K

See also Harbour Works and Dredging Craft

BLYTH TUG CO LTD

Blyth

FUNNEL: Yellow with blue Maltese cross.
HULL: Black.
AREA OF OPERATION: Blyth.

Name	Built	Tons Gross	Horse Power	Engines
Maximus	1956	141	750(B)	M/K

Top: PETER LEIGH, F. A. Ashmead & Sons Ltd *P. L. White*

CHARLOCK, Braithwaite & Dean Ltd *M. J. Gaston*

PORT OF BOSTON AUTHORITY

Boston, Lincs.

FUNNEL: White with black top.
HULL: Black with red boot-topping.
AREA OF OPERATION: Boston, Lincs.

Name	Built	Tons Gross	Horse Power	Engines
Bostonian	1967	50	528(B)	M

See also Harbour Works and Dredging Craft

BOSTON DEEP SEA FISHERIES LTD

Lowestoft

FUNNEL: None.
HULL: Black with white line and red boot-topping.
AREA OF OPERATION: Lowestoft.

Name	Built	Tons Gross	Horse Power	Engines
Columbus ex Wilhelmina 8-69	1954	35	350(B)	M
Corlea	1933	31	110(B)	M

See also Trawlers

BRAITHWAITE & DEAN LTD

London

FUNNEL: White with black lip.
HULL: Black with white topline and red boot-topping separated by white line.
AREA OF OPERATION: River Thames (Lighterage).

Name	Built	Tons Gross	Horse Power	Engines
Charlock	1962	42	385(B)	M

BRITISH RAILWAYS BOARD

London

FUNNEL: White with black top, with British Rail "Twin Arrow" symbol on wheel-house.
HULL: Blue with red boot-topping.
AREA OF OPERATION: Newhaven.

Name	Built	Tons Gross	Horse Power	Engines
Meeching	1960	160	1.040(B)	M

See also Coastal Ships

BRITISH TRANSPORT DOCKS BOARD

London

FUNNEL: Blue, with or without black top and white "Bollard" symbol.
HULL: Black.
AREA OF OPERATION: Fleetwood, Hull and Newport.

Name	Built	Tons Gross	Horse Power	Engines
Llanwern	1960	152	1,200(B)	DE(2)
Newport	1956	139	700(B)	M
St. Woolas	1960	152	1,200(B)	M(2)
Wyke*	1956	62	480(B)	M

* Converted for survey work 1972
See also Harbour Works and Dredging Cra⁴t

BRITISH WATERWAYS BOARD

Gloucester, Goole & London

FUNNEL: Black with blue "Wave" symbol on broad white band.
HULL: Black with white line and blue topsides.
AREA OF OPERATION: Gloucester & Sharpness Canal and Inland Waterways from Goole & London.

Name	Built	Tons Gross	Horse Power	Engines
Gloucester & Sharpness Canal Fleet:				
Primrose	1906	52	204(B)	M rbt fm SR

British Waterways Board (Continued)

Name	Built	Tons Gross	Horse Power	Engines
Severn Active	1904	53	204(B)	M rbt fm SR
Speedwell	1968	50	330(B)	M
Stanegarth	1910	47	204(B)	M rbt fm SR
Goole Fleet:				
Allerton Bywater	1960	53	135(B)	M
Brodsworth	1960	53	135(B)	M
Freight Pioneer	1970		300(B)	M/Pusher
Freight Trader	1971		300(B)	M/Pusher
Hatfield	1959	53	135(B)	M
Water Haigh	1960	53	135(B)	M
West Riding	1958	53	135(B)	M
London Fleet:				
Freight Endeavour ex Placer-74	1967	38	420(B)	M/Pusher
Freight Mover ex Plausible-74	1968	38	420(B)	M/Pusher

T. R. BROWN & SONS LTD

Bristol

FUNNEL: Black with broad red band between narrow white bands.
HULL: Black with white line.
AREA OF OPERATION: Avonmouth, Bristol and Bristol Channel (Lighterage).

Name	Built	Tons Gross	Horse Power	Engines
Ernest Brown ex Tid-95	1944	54	220(B)	M rbt fm SR

See also Coastal Ships

BULK CARGO HANDLING SERVICES LTD
(A Subsidiary of the Alexandra Towing Co Ltd)

Liverpool

FUNNEL: Black with red letters "BCHS" on red bordered white panel on broad blue band between narrow blue bands.
HULL: Black with red boot-topping.
AREA OF OPERATION: River Mersey (Lighterage).

Name	Built	Tons Gross	Horse Power	Engines
Cherry ex Cherrygarth-72	1963	62	400(B)	M

See also Coastal Ships

CAWOOD HARGREAVES LTD

Hull

FUNNEL: None.
HULL: Black.
AREA OF OPERATION: Inland waterways from Hull & Goole.

Name	Built	Tons Gross	Horse Power	Engines
CH 106	1967	60	150(B)	M/Pusher
CH 107	1967	60	150(B)	M/Pusher
CH 108	1967	60	150(B)	M/Pusher
CH 109	1967	60	150(B)	M/Pusher

CLEMENTS-TOUGH, LTD
(Dickinson Robinson Group)

London

FUNNEL: Cream with narrow red band and red letters "DRG" in red ring.
HULL: Black with white line and red boot-topping.
AREA OF OPERATION: River Thames (Lighterage).

Name	Built	Tons Gross	Horse Power	Engines
Fenland ex Seaby	1929	38	400(B)	M rbt fm SR
Ham	1925	44	240(B)	M rbt fm SR
Sheen	1925	52	300(B)	M rbt fm SR

CLYDE SHIPPING CO LTD

Glasgow

FUNNEL: Black.
HULL: Black with dummy black ports on broad red ochre band with white line above.
AREA OF OPERATION: River Clyde and UK, Irish Coastal Towage.

Name	Built	Tons Gross	Horse Power	Engines
Flying Demon	1964	131	1,000(B)	M
Flying Dipper	1958	274	1,200(B)	M
Flying Duck	1956	176	1,040(B)	M
Flying Falcon	1968	230	1,470(B)	M/K/FF
Flying Foam	1962	184	1,350(B)	M
Flying Fulmar	1973	299	2,800(B)	M/SAL/FF
Flying Mist	1962	184	1,350(B)	M
Flying Scout	1970	290	2,800(B)	M/K
Flying Spray	1962	184	1,350(B)	M
New	1975		2,640(B)	M

COLNE FISHING CO LTD

Lowestoft

FUNNEL: Blue with black top.
HULL: Black.
AREA OF OPERATION: Lowestoft.

Name	Built	Tons Gross	Horse Power	Engines
Ala ex Sean Clair-74 Pinegarth-72	1961	61	400(B)	M

See also Trawlers

Wm. CORY & SON LTD
(A division of Ocean Transport & Trading Ltd)

FUNNEL: Black with black diamond on white band.
HULL: Black with white or silver line and red boot-topping.
AREA OF OPERATION: As below.

Name	Built	Tons Gross	Horse Power	Engines
Cory Ship Towage Ltd (Avonmouth, Bristol, Cardiff, Barry, Newport, Milford Haven, Plymouth, Cobh and UK and Irish Coastal Towage):				
Anglegarth	1960	306	1,300(B)	M/SAL/K

Top: FLYING FALCON, Clyde Shipping Co Ltd *J. K. Byass*

WESTGARTH, Cory Ship Towage Ltd *'Fotoship'*

Wm. Cory & Son Ltd (Continued)

Name	Built	Tons Gross	Horse Power	Engines
Avongarth	1960	156	960(B)	M
Bargarth	1966	161	850(B)	M/K
Butegarth	1966	161	850(B)	M/K
Dalegarth	1960	306	1,300(B)	M/SAL/K
Danegarth	1966	161	850(B)	M/K
Falgarth	1958	102	500(B)	M/K
ex Cleddia-62				
Glengarth	1970	292	2,460(B)	M/FF/K
Graygarth	1970	291	2,460(B)	M/FF/K
Greengarth	1970	291	2,460(B)	M/FF/K
Gwentgarth	1962	186	1,320(B)	M
ex Dunsnipe-71				
Lowgarth	1965	152	850(B)	M/K
Pengarth	1962	160	1,080(B)	M
Plymgarth	1958	208	800(B)	M
ex Thunderer-73				
Polgarth	1962	160	1,080(B)	M
Portgarth	1959	207	1,260(B)	M
ex Cashèl-73				
Ramsgarth	1964	306	1,300(B)	M/K
Rathgarth	1965	306	1,300(B)	M/K
Reagarth	1964	306	1,300(B)	M/K
Stackgarth*	1959	306	1,300(B)	M/K
Thorngarth*	1959	306	1,300(B)	M/K
Uskgarth	1966	161	850(B)	M/K
Westgarth	1962	186	1,320(B)	M
ex Duncurlew-71				
New (2)	1975/76	300	2,520(B)	M/FF/K
New (4)	1975/76	300	2,520(B)	M/K

Bantry Bay Towing Co Ltd (Bantry Bay and S. Irish Coastal Towage):

Name	Built	Tons Gross	Horse Power	Engines
Bantry Bay	1968	299	2,500(B)	M/FF
Brandon Bay	1968	299	2,500(B)	M/FF
Dingle Bay	1968	299	2,500(B)	M/FF
Tralee Bay	1968	299	2,500(B)	M/FF

Cory Ship Towage (Clyde) Ltd (Clyde area and UK and Irish Coastal Towage):

Name	Built	Tons Gross	Horse Power	Engines
Brigadier	1961	223	1,020(B)	M
Campaigner	1957	248	1,065(B)	M
Chieftain	1968	205	1,650(B)	M/K
Cruiser	1959	207	1,260(B)	M/FF/K
ex Clonmel-73				
Strongbow	1961	225	1,020(B)	M
Thunderer	1970	272	2,400(B)	M/K
ex Warrior-73				
Vanguard	1964	224	1,020(B)	M
Wrestler	1957	248	1,065(B)	M

Cory Ship Towage (N.I.) Ltd (Belfast, Londonderry, UK and Irish Coastal Towage):

Name	Built	Tons Gross	Horse Power	Engines
Carrickfergus	1958	161	960(B)	M
Clandeboye	1967	167	1,260(B)	M/FF/K
Coleraine	1970	212	1,260(B)	M
Craigdarragh	1966	169	1,260(B)	M

* Registered at Cork and operating in that area

Wm. Cory & Son Ltd (Continued)

Name	Built	Tons Gross	Horse Power	Engines
Cultra	1962	202	1,260(B)	M
Dunosprey	1968	173	1,380(B)	M

Cory Lighterage Ltd (River Thames (Lighterage)):

Name	Built	Tons Gross	Horse Power	Engines
Dockman† ex Stamford Brook	1949	68	520(B)	M
Merit ex Lingo	1964	83	627(B)	M
Mercedes II ex Silverbeam-71	1951	92	605(B)	M
Recruit	1952	91	670(B)	M
Redoubt	1916	71	440(B)	M rbt fm SR
Regard	1958	69	403(B)	M
Relentless	1943	61	450(B)	M
Revenge	1948	61	528(B)	M
Swiftstone	1952	91	670(B)	M
Touchstone	1962	75	528(B)	M

Mercantile Lighterage Ltd (River Thames (Lighterage)):

Name	Built	Tons Gross	Horse Power	Engines
Hawkstone	1948	61	450(B)	M
Hurricane	1938	90	550(B)	M
Mersina ex Repulse	1955	79	670(B)	M

† *To be renamed REGAL*

See also Coastal Ships and Rea Towing Co Ltd

W. G. S. CROUCH & SONS LTD

Greenhithe

FUNNEL: Yellow with blue over white over red over white over blue bands.
HULL: Black.
AREA OF OPERATION: River Thames (Lighterage and Contract Work).

Name	Built	Tons Gross	Horse Power	Engines
Lads Spearing ex Vange-71	1936	38	375(B)	M

See also Coastal Ships

W. R. CUNIS LTD

London

FUNNEL: White with black top separated by narrow white over red bands.
HULL: Black with red boot-topping.
AREA OF OPERATION: River Thames (Lighterage).

Name	Built	Tons Gross	Horse Power	Engines
William Ryan ex Toro	1908	72	530(B)	M rbt fm SR
Tom Jay	1945	67	408(B)	M

DARLING BROS. LTD

London

FUNNEL: White with green pyramid.
HULL: Black with two white lines and red boot-topping separated by a white line.
AREA OF OPERATION: River Thames (Lighterage).

Name	Built	Tons Gross	Horse Power	Engines
Arthur Darling ex John Hawkins-69	1946	50	275(B)	M

M. G. DEAL

Southend

FUNNEL:
HULL:
AREA OF OPERATION: Contract Work, River Thames and S.E. Coast.

Name	Built	Tons Gross	Horse Power	Engines
Eugenio	1957		300(B)	M

J. DINWOODIE & CO

Granton

FUNNEL: Brown with black top.
HULL: Black with white line and red boot-topping.
AREA OF OPERATION: Granton.

Name	Built	Tons Gross	Horse Power	Engines
Inchkeith	1940	39	150(B)	M
Inchmickry	1946	39	175(B)	M
ex Thames Pilot-67				

DOVER HARBOUR BOARD

Dover

FUNNEL: None.
HULL: Black with white line and green boot-topping.
AREA OF OPERATION: Dover and English Channel.

Name	Built	Tons Gross	Horse Power	Engines
Diligent	1957	161	1,040(B)	M(2)
Dominant	1958	161	1,008(B)	M(2)

See also Harbour Works and Dredging Craft

ERITH & DARTFORD LIGHTERAGE CO LTD

Erith

FUNNEL: Black with white "ED" monogram.
HULL: Dark green with red boot-topping.
AREA OF OPERATION: River Thames (Lighterage).

Name	Built	Tons Gross	Horse Power	Engines
Caroline	1937	50	340(B)	M rbt fm SR
ex Isleworth Lion-65, General V				

F. T. EVERARD & SONS LTD

Greenhithe

FUNNEL: Black with red and white diagonally quartered houseflag.
HULL: Black with white line and red boot-topping.
AREA OF OPERATION: River Thames (Lighterage) Ship towage of Company's vessels on South East Coast.

Name	Built	Tons Gross	Horse Power	Engines
Capable ex Platonic-74	1968	38	420(B)	M
P. B. Everard ex Margaret Locket-70	1951	74	450(B)	M
R. A. Everard ex Pinklake	1943	87	760(B)	M
S. A. Everard	1939	124	800(B)	M

See also Coastal Ships

FALMOUTH TOWAGE CO LTD

Falmouth

FUNNEL: Black with broad white band.
HULL: Green with black topsides separated by a white line and red boot-topping.
AREA OF OPERATION: Falmouth.

Name	Built	Tons Gross	Horse Power	Engines
St. Agnes ex Warrior-68	1935	251	1,200(B)	M rbt fm SR
St. Denys ex Northgate Scot-59	1929	174	790(I)	SR
St. Eval ex Chieftain-67	1930	196	660(B)	M rbt fm SR
St. Mawes ex Arusha-59	1951	346	800(I)	SR
St. Merryn ex Rockpigeon	1945	233	1,000(I)	SR

FELIXARC LTD

Felixstowe

FUNNEL: Blue with blue "FA" monogram on yellow band.
HULL: Black.
AREA OF OPERATION: Felixstowe.

Name	Built	Tons Gross	Horse Power	Engines
Felix-tow	1957		200(B)	M

DAVID FERRAN & SONS

Belfast

FUNNEL: Yellow with black top.
HULL: Black with red boot-topping.
AREA OF OPERATION: Belfast (Contract Work).

Name	Built	Tons Gross	Horse Power	Engines
David Ferran ex Sir Kenneth-72	1958	67	330(B)	M(2)

FLEETWOOD FISHING VESSEL OWNERS ASSOCIATION

Fleetwood

FUNNEL:
HULL:
AREA OF OPERATION: Fleetwood.

Name	Built	Tons Gross	Horse Power	Engines
Finch ex Boys White-69, Falconbrook-67	1956	58	310(B)	M

FORTH PORTS AUTHORITY

Leith

FUNNEL: Black.
HULL: Black with white line and red boot-topping.
AREA OF OPERATION: Leith and Firth of Forth.

Name	Built	Tons Gross	Horse Power	Engines
Craigleith	1958	183	818(B)	M/K
Gunnet	1967	143	1,200(B)	M(2)/VS
Incholm	1967	143	1,200(B)	M(2)/VS
Martello	1958	68	440(B)	M/K

See also Harbour Works and Dredging Craft

FOWEY HARBOUR COMMISSIONERS

Fowey

FUNNEL: Yellow with black top.
HULL: Green with black topsides and red boot-topping.
AREA OF OPERATION: Fowey.

Name	Built	Tons Gross	Horse Power	Engines
Cannis ex Enticette-65	1953	91	600(B)	M
Gribbin Head ex Ingleby Cross-68	1955	132	750(B)	M

FRANCE, FENWICK TYNE & WEAR CO LTD

Newcastle

FUNNEL: Light blue with black top separated by broad band of blue and white vertical stripes with a blue anchor superimposed.
HULL: Black with yellow lines and green boot-topping.
AREA OF OPERATION: Sunderland and River Wear. (The company's tugs also work in the colours of Tyne Tugs Ltd on the River Tyne.)

Name	Built	Tons Gross	Horse Power	Engines
Cornhill	1943	176	750(B)	M
Dunelm	1964	150	986(B)	M

Top: TOUCHSTONE, Cory Lighterage Ltd *M. J. Gaston*

FORTH, Grangemouth & Forth Towing Co Ltd '*Fotoship*'

195

France, Fenwick Tyne & Wear Co Ltd (Continued)

Name	Built	Tons Gross	Horse Power	Engines
Marsden	1956	122	1,080(B)	M
Prestwick	1955	119	1,080(B)	M
Whitburn	1943	176	750(B)	M
ex Kronos-64				

GASELEE (FELIXSTOWE) LTD

Greenwich

FUNNEL: Yellow with three narrow red bands and Dick & Page houseflag superimposed.
HULL: Black with white line and red boot-topping.
AREA OF OPERATION: Felixstowe, Harwich and South East Coast.

Name	Built	Tons Gross	Horse Power	Engines
Sauria	1968	165	1,340(B)	M/FF

GILYOTT & SCOTT LTD

Hull

FUNNEL: Yellow with black letter "G" or yellow with black top.
HULL: Black.
AREA OF OPERATION: River Humber and surrounding waterways (Lighter-age).

Name	Built	Tons Gross	Horse Power	Engines
Gillian Knight	1956	32	250(B)	M
Hippo D.	1931	45	220(B)	M rbt fm SR
ex Lion H.				

GRANGEMOUTH & FORTH TOWING CO LTD

Grangemouth

FUNNEL: Yellow with black top.
HULL: Black with red boot-topping.
AREA OF OPERATION: Grangemouth and Firth of Forth.

Name	Built	Tons Gross	Horse Power	Engines
Carron	1960	116	1,060(B)	M
ex Flying Witch-73				
Dalgrain	1963	129	840(B)	M
Forth	1967	184	1,140(B)	M
Zetland	1961	138	840(B)	M
New (2)	1975	300	2,640(B)	M/FF
New (2)	1975	300	2,640(B)	M

GRAVESEND TOWING CO LTD

Gravesend

FUNNEL: Green with broad white band.
HULL: Black.
AREA OF OPERATION: River Thames (Lighterage).

Name	Built	Tons Gross	Horse Power	Engines
General IV	1936	50	390(B)	M
Tudorose	1936		580(B)	M
Union	1895	48	300(B)	M rbt fm SR

GREAT YARMOUTH PORT AND HAVEN COMMISSIONERS

Great Yarmouth

FUNNEL: Black with Commissioners armorial shield in full colour.
HULL: Black with white line and red boot-topping.
AREA OF OPERATION: Great Yarmouth.

Name	Built	Tons Gross	Horse Power	Engines
Hector Reed	1966	65	590(B)	M

GREENHITHE LIGHTERAGE CO LTD

Greenhithe

FUNNEL: Yellow.
HULL: Green with white line and red boot-topping.
AREA OF OPERATION: River Thames (Lighterage).

Name	Built	Tons Gross	Horse Power	Engines
Britannia ex T. B. Heathorne	1893	76	360(B)	M rbt fm SR

See also Coastal Ships

GRIMSBY SALVAGE & TOWING CO LTD

Grimsby

FUNNEL: Cream with red letters "GST" on white band between narrow red bands separating black top.
HULL: Black with red boot-topping.
AREA OF OPERATION: Grimsby.

Name	Built	Tons Gross	Horse Power	Engines
Alfred Bannister	1964	35	360(B)	M
Brenda Fisher	1955	52	360(B)	M
Herbert Crampin	1966	44	451(B)	M
Sir Jack Croft Baker	1964	35	360(B)	M
Sir John Marsden	1964	35	360(B)	M
Thomas Baskcomb	1963	35	360(B)	M
William Grant	1963	35	360(B)	M

HOLYHEAD TOWING CO LTD
(Holyhead Salvage Co Ltd)

Holyhead

FUNNEL: Red with Company symbol in white.
HULL: Black with red boot-topping.
AREA OF OPERATION: Holyhead and Continental, UK and Irish Coastal Towage and Salvage.

Name	Built	Tons Gross	Horse Power	Engines
Afon Las ex Onset-73, M.S.C. Onset-73	1948	154	1,200(B)	M(2)

Top: HECTOR READ, Great Yarmouth Port & Haven Commiss. *'Fotoship'*

WILLIAM GRANT, Grimsby Salvage & Towage Co Ltd *T. J. M. Wood*

Holyhead Towing Co Ltd (Continued)

Name	Built	Tons Gross	Horse Power	Engines
Afon Wen ex Plateau-73	1952	159	1,200(B)	M

JOHN HOWARD & CO (NORTHERN) LTD

London & Liverpool

FUNNEL: Green with large white letter "H".
HULL: Black with red boot-topping.
AREA OF OPERATION: Contract work and Coastal Towage.

Name	Built	Tons Gross	Horse Power	Engines
Kinghow ex Charles Hearn-67	1959	139	740(B)	M(2)
Argon Investments Ltd; Hamilton, Bermuda:				
Alison Howard II	1972	150		M
Howard Marine & Dredging Co Ltd·				
Susie Howard	1973	148		M

THE HULL STEAM TRAWLERS MUTUAL INSURANCE & PROTECTING CO LTD

Hull

FUNNEL: Yellow with black top.
HULL: Black.
AREA OF OPERATION: Hull Fish Docks.

Name	Built	Tons Gross	Horse Power	Engines
Aurora	1963	50	385(B)	M/VS
Neptune	1966	50	385(B)	M/VS
Triton	1964	50	385(B)	M/VS
Zephyr	1964	50	385(B)	M/VS

HUMBER TUGS LTD
(Subsidiary of United Towing Ltd)

Grimsby, Hull, Immingham

FUNNEL: Black with two white bands.
HULL: Black with white line and green boot-topping or grey with black topsides and yellow line with green boot-topping.
AREA OF OPERATION: Hull and River Humber, Grimsby, Immingham and Coastal Towage when required.

Name	Built	Tons Gross	Horse Power	Engines
Riverman	1955	37	420(B)	M
ex Bargeman-74, Brentonian-65				
Headman	1963	193	1,750(B)	M(2)
Keelman	1958	37	420(B)	M
ex Scorcher-65				
Lady Alma	1966	218	2,024(B)	M(2)
Lady Cecilia	1966	198	2,024(B)	M(2)
Lady Elsie	1970	263	2,800(B)	M/K
Lady Laura	1967	114	1,240(B)	M
Lady Marina	1967	114	1,240(B)	M
Lady Sarah	1970	263	2,800(B)	M/K
Lady Sybil	1965	111	797(B)	M
Lady Thelma	1967	211	2,024(B)	M/FF
Lady Theresa	1967	261	2,400(B)	M(2)SAL
ex Yorkshireman-74				
Lady Vera	1972	263	2.460(B)	M/K
Lighterman	1954	37	420(B)	M
ex Jaycee-65				
Motorman	1965	98	900(B)	M
Tidesman	1963	98	792(B)	M(2)
Trawlerman	1963	98	792(B)	M(2)
Tugman	1964	98	792(B)	M(2)
Waterman	1966	48	480(B)	M(2)
Workman	1963	193	1,750(B)	M(2)
New(2)	1974/75			M(2)

See also United Towing (Ocean Tugs) Ltd

HUMPHREY & GREY (LIGHTERAGE) LTD

London

FUNNEL: Black with red band bordered by yellow bands.
HULL: Black with white line and red boot-topping.
AREA OF OPERATION: River Thames (Lighterage).

Name	Built	Tons Gross	Horse Power	Engines
Friston Down	1964	99	650(B)	M

Humphrey & Grey (Lighterage) Ltd (Continued)

Name	Built	Tons Gross	Horse Power	Engines
Owen Smith ex Fossa-61	1946	66	450(B)	M
Sir Aubrey	1962	59	450(B)	M
Sir John	1935	83	500(B)	M rbt fm SR
St. Olaf	1956	37	360(B)	M

HUSBAND'S SHIPYARDS LTD

Southampton

FUNNEL: Yellow with houseflag. (Divided vertically, black, white, red, with black letter "H" on white.)
HULL: Black with red boot-topping separated by white line.
AREA OF OPERATION: Southampton Water, Solent and local Sea Areas.

Name	Built	Tons Gross	Horse Power	Engines
Abundance	1950	65	400(B)	M
Adherence ex Tid 75.-65	1944	54	400(B)	M rbt fm SR
Affluence ex C. 10	1938	91	450(B)	M
Assurance ex Tid 71-65	1944	54	450(B)	M rbt fm SR

IRVINE HARBOUR COMPANY

Irvine

FUNNEL: Maroon with black top.
HULL: Black with red boot-topping.
AREA OF OPERATION: Irvine.

Name	Built	Tons Gross	Horse Power	Engines
Garnock	1956	78	324(B)	(M/K)

Top: FRISTON DOWN, Humphrey & Grey (Lighterage) Ltd *M. J. Gaston*

SEA BRISTOLIAN, C. J. King & Sons (Tugs) Ltd '*Fotoship*'

ITCHEN MARINE TOWAGE LTD

Southampton

FUNNEL: Red with black top separated by blue band.
HULL: Black with red boot-topping.
AREA OF OPERATION: Southampton (Lighterage).

Name	Built	Tons Gross	Horse Power	Engines
Testgarth	1937	60	390(B)	M

KIER LTD

Poole

FUNNEL: Black with "KIER" in blue on broad white band.
HULL: Black with white line and red boot-topping.
AREA OF OPERATION: Contract work, Milford Haven.

Name	Built	Tons Gross	Horse Power	Engines
Sheilia ex Wachtel	1940	52	460(B)	M

C. J. KING & SONS (TUGS) LTD

Bristol

FUNNEL: White with black top separated by broad orange band.
HULL: Black with yellow line.
AREA OF OPERATION: Avonmouth, Bristol and Bristol Channel.

Name	Built	Tons Gross	Horse Power	Engines
Sea Alert	1960	168	600(B)	M
Sea Bristolian ex Foreman-72	1959	227	1,250(B)	M
Sea Challenge	1967	185	1,100(B)	M
Sea Merrimac	1964	163	920(B)	M
Sea Volunteer	1963	163	920(B)	M

THE KING'S LYNN CONSERVANCY BOARD

King's Lynn

FUNNEL: Yellow with black top.
HULL: Grey with white line and red boot-topping.
AREA OF OPERATION: King's Lynn.

Name	Built	Tons Gross	Horse Power	Engines
Conservator K. L.	1963	42	350(B)	M

J. P. KNIGHT LTD

Rochester

FUNNEL: Black with two white bands above white letter "K".
HULL: Black with white topline and red boot-topping.
AREA OF OPERATION: Isle of Grain, River Medway, occasionally River Thames and short Coastal Towage. Also at Ivergordon.

Name	Built	Tons Gross	Horse Power	Engines
Kelvedon	1940	41	300(B)	M
ex Keston-69				
Kemsing	1960	135	1,000(B)	M
Kenley	1958	246	1,500(B)	M/FF
Kennet	1965	278	1,810(B)	M/K
Kent	1948	121	850(B)	M
Keston	1970	300	3,000(B)	M(3)K/FF
Kestrel	1955	223	1,150(B)	M/FF
Kessock	1974	220		M/FF
Keverne	1960	247	1,650(B)	M/K/FF
Kinlock	1974	220		M
Kite	1952	118	950(B)	M
Knighton	1968	276	1,810(B)	M/K

See also Coastal Ships

LIVERPOOL GRAIN STORAGE & TRANSIT CO LTD

Liverpool

FUNNEL: Blue with yellow grain sheaf emblem.
HULL: Black with white line.
AREA OF OPERATION: River Mersey (Lighterage).

Name	Built	Tons Gross	Horse Power	Engines
Castor ex Tidworth-66 Tid 116	1944	54	400(B)	M rbt fm SR
Ceres	1961	43	400(B)	M

LONDON & ROCHESTER TRADING CO LTD

Rochester

FUNNEL: Black with silver crescent on broad red band between narrow white bands.
HULL: Light brown with two white lines and red boot-topping.
AREA OF OPERATION: River Medway (Lighterage). Ship towage of Company's vessels on South East Coast.

Name	Built	Tons Gross	Horse Power	Engines
Dragette	1947	50	300(B)	M
Lashette	1971	157	730(B)	M(2)SCH
Luggette ex Superbe-73	1959	116	650(B)	M

See also Coastal Ships

LONDON TUGS LTD

London

FUNNEL: Black with Dick & Page houseflag on broad red band between two narrow white bands.
HULL: Black with white topline and red boot-topping.
AREA OF OPERATION: River Thames, Felixstowe and Coastal Towage.

Name	Built	Tons Gross	Horse Power	Engines
Avenger	1962	300	2,250(B)	M/K
Burma	1966	166	1,050(B)	M

Name	Built	Tons Gross	Horse Power	Engines
Dhulia	1959	272	1,600(B)	M
Fossa	1961	83	1,000(B)	M
Hibernia	1963	293	1,800(B)	M/K/FF
Ionia*	1960	120	1,360(B)	M
Moorcock	1959	273	1,600(B)	M
Rana*	1951	99	700(B)	M
Sun II	1965	150	1,350(B)	M
Sun III	1966	150	1,350(B)	M
Sun XVIII	1951	105	560(B)	M
Sun XIX	1956	192	1,170(B)	M
Sun XX	1957	192	1,170(B)	M
Sun XXI	1959	183	1,400(B)	M
Sun XXII	1960	183	1,400(B)	M
Sun XXIV	1962	113	720(B)	M
Sun XXV	1963	230	1,810(B)	M/K/FF
Sun XXVI	1965	230	1,810(B)	M/K/FF
Sun XXVII	1968	226	1,810(B)	M/K/FF
Vanquisher	1955	294	1,280(B)	M
Watercock	1967	161	1,050(B)	M

* *Working at Felixstowe in conjunction with Gaselee (Felixstowe) Ltd*

M. B. DREDGING CO LTD

London

FUNNEL: Grey with houseflag (White edged blue pennant containing white letters "MBD").
HULL: Dark Grey.
AREA OF OPERATION: River Thames or on contract work.

Name	Built	Tons Gross	Horse Power	Engines
Melhuish	1957	47	400(B)	M
Pushman	1970	38	574(B)	M/Pusher
Thrush ex Teal, Gull	1952	75	400(B)	M

MANCHESTER SHIP CANAL CO LTD

Manchester

FUNNEL: Black with two white bands.
HULL: Black.
AREA OF OPERATION: Manchester Docks and Ship Canal.

Name	Built	Tons Gross	Horse Power	Engines
M.S.C. Onward	1948	154	1,200(B)	M(2)
M.S.C. Panther	1950	154	1,200(B)	M(2)
M.S.C. Puma	1950	154	1,200(B)	M(2)
M.S.C. Quarry	1951	154	1,200(B)	M(2)
M.S.C. Quest	1951	154	1,200(B)	M(2)
M.S.C. Ranger	1952	154	1,200(B)	M(2)
M.S.C. Rover	1952	154	1,200(B)	M(2)
M.S.C. Sabre	1956	147	1,290(B)	M(2)
M.S.C. Sceptre	1956	147	1,290(B)	M(2)
M.S.C. Scimitar	1956	147	1,290(B)	M(2)
M.S.C. Sovereign	1957	147	1,290(B)	M(2)
M.S.C. Talisman	1961	124	1,210(B)	M(2)
M.S.C. Tarn	1961	124	1,210(B)	M(2)
M.S.C. Ulex	1965	127	1,300(B)	M(2)
M.S.C. Undine	1965	127	1,300(B)	M(2)
M.S.C. Viceroy	1974	125	1,200(B)	M(2)
M.S.C. Victory	1974	125	1,200(B)	M(2)
New (2)	1975/76	125	1,200(B)	M(2)
Dredging Fleet Tugs:				
M.S.C. Dainty	1959	37	140(B)	M
M.S.C. Daphne	1954	83	140(B)	M
M.S.C. Daring	1959	37	140(B)	M
M.S.C. Dawn	1960	37	140(B)	M
M.S.C. Deborah	1958	35	140(B)	M
M.S.C. Diana	1956	84	140(B)	M
M.S.C. Dido	1959	35	140(B)	M

See also Harbour Works and Dredging Craft

W. G. MARRIOTT

London

FUNNEL: Cream with narrow black top.
HULL: Black.
AREA OF OPERATION: River Thames (Lighterage).

Name	Built	Tons Gross	Horse Power	Engines
William George	1949			M

Top: KESTON, J. P. Knight Ltd *M. J. Gaston*

M.S.C. DAPHNE, Manchester Ship Canal Co Ltd *J. Clarkson*

McCANN TUGS LTD

London

FUNNEL: Blue with black and blue letter "M" interrupting blue band between white bands.
HULL: Black with red boot-topping.
AREA OF OPERATION: River Thames (Lighterage).

Name	Built	Tons Gross	Horse Power	Engines
A.P.M. ex H.R.M.-72, Albion-64, Thames	1924		560(B)	M rbt fm SR
Cabot	1952	98	400(B)	M
General VI ex Mick, Caledonian	1946	50	390(B)	M
Lily White ex Balna	1929	38	300(B)	M
Wortha	1929	96	360(B)	M rbt fm SR

C. METCALFE

Birkenhead

FUNNEL: Blue with black and white "CM" monogram on black bordered blue shield superimposed on broad white band and narrow black top.
HULL: Black with red boot-topping.
AREA OF OPERATION: Contract Work, North West Coast.

Name	Built	Tons Gross	Horse Power	Engines
Trover ex Sunnyside, Tid 59	1944	54	450(B)	M rbt fm SR

MINISTRY OF DEFENCE (NAVY)
(Royal Maritime Auxiliary Service)

London

FUNNEL: Grey with black top.
HULL: Black.
AREA OF OPERATION: Worldwide Towage of Royal Naval Ships and Support Craft and Salvage Operations.

Name	Built	Tons Gross	Horse Power	Engines
Cyclone	1942	1,100	3,020(B)	M/SAL
ex Welshman-65,				
Castle Peak-62,				
Caroline Moller-54,				
Growler-52				
Eminent	1946	295	800(B)	SR
Robust*	1971	900	4,500(B)	M(2)/SAL/FF
Rollicker	1970	900	4,500(B)	M(2)/SAL/FF
Roysterer	1971	900	4,500(B)	M(2)/SAL/FF
Typhoon	1958	1,034	2,880(B)	M/SAL/FF

* *Presently manned by P.A.S personnel*

MINISTRY OF DEFENCE (NAVY)
(Port Auxiliary Service)

London

FUNNEL: Yellow with black top with white bordered or plain blue band.
HULL: Black with blue or white line and red boot-topping.
AREA OF OPERATION: Chatham, Clyde, Devonport, Portland, Portsmouth, Rosyth and overseas bases.

Name	Built	Tons Gross	Horse Power	Engines
Accord	1957	760	1,600(B)	M(2)/SAL
Advice	1957	760	1,600(B)	M(2)/SAL
Agatha	1961	38	400(B)	M
Agile	1958	641	1,600(B)	M(2)/SAL
Agnes	1961	38	400(B)	M
Airedale	1961	152	1,320(B)	M(2)
Alice	1961	38	400(B)	M
Alsation	1961	152	1,320(B)	M(2)
Audrey	1961	38	400(B)	M
Barbara	1963	38	400(B)	M
Basset	1963	152	1,320(B)	M(2)
ex Beagle-68				
Betty	1963	38	400(B)	M
Boxer	1963	152	1,320(B)	M(2)

Name	Built	Tons Gross	Horse Power	Engines
Brenda	1963	38	400(B)	M
Bridget	1963	38	400(B)	M
Cairn	1964	152	1,320(B)	M(2)
Charlotte	1968	69	650(B)	M
Christine	1968	69	650(B)	M
Clare	1968	69	650(B)	M
Collie	1964	152	1,320(B)	M(2)
Confiance	1955	760	1,600(B)	M(2)/SAL
Confident	1956	760	1,600(B)	M(2)/SAL
Corgi	1964	152	1,320(B)	M(2)
Daisy	1968	69	650(B)	M
Dalmation	1965	152	1,320(B)	M(2)
Daphne	1968	69	650(B)	M
Deerhound	1965	152	1,320(B)	M(2)
Dexterous	1957	473	1,600(B)	DE(PW)/FF
Director	1957	473	1,600(B)	DE(PW)/FF
Doris	1969	69	650(B)	M
Dorothy	1968	69	650(B)	M
Elkhound	1965	152	1,320(B)	M(2)
Faithful	1957	473	1,600(B)	DE(PW)/FF
Favourite	1958	473	1,600(B)	DE(PW)/FF
Felicity	1968	72	600(B)	M/VS
Fiona	1973	50	330(B)	M/VS
Forceful	1957	473	1,600(B)	DE(PW)/FF
Georgina	1973	50	330(B)	M/VS
Grinder	1958	473	1,600(B)	DE(PW)/FF
Griper	1958	473	1,600(B)	DE(PW)/FF
Gwendoline	1974	50	330(B)	M/VS
Helen	1973	50	330(B)	M/VS
Husky	1969	152	1,320(B)	M(2)
Irene	1972	50	330(B)	M/VS
Isabel	1972	50	330(B)	M/VS
Jean	1972	50	330(B)	M/VS
Joan	1972	50	330(B)	M/VS
Joyce	1972	50	330(B)	M/VS
Kathleen	1972	50	330(B)	M/VS
Kitty	1972	50	330(B)	M/VS
Labrador	1966	152	1,320(B)	M(2)
Lesley	1973	50	330(B)	M/VS
Lilah	1973	50	330(B)	M/VS
Mary	1973	50	330(B)	M/VS
Mastiff	1968	152	1,320(B)	M(2)
May	1973	50	330(B)	M/VS
Myrtle	1973	50	330(B)	M/VS
Nancy	1973	50	330(B)	M/VS
Norah	1973	50	330(B)	M/VS
Pointer	1966	152	1,320(B)	M(2)
Prompt ex Warden-51, Empire Spitfire-47	1943	232	900(I)	SR
Saluki	1968	152	1,320(B)	M(2)
Samson	1954	855	3,000(I)	SR(2)/SAL
Sea Giant	1955	855	3,000(I)	SR(2)/SAL
Sealyham	1968	152	1,320(B)	M(2)
Setter	1969	152	1,320(B)	M(2)

Top: DAPHNE, Ministry of Defence (Navy) *M.O.D. (Navy)*

IRENE, Ministry of Defence (Navy) *M.O.D. (Navy)*

Name	Built	Tons Gross	Horse Power	Engines
Sheepdog	1968	152	1,320(B)	M(2)
Spaniel	1968	152	1,320(B)	M(2)
Superman	1954	855	3,000(B)	SR(2)/SAL
Tanac 83	1944	55	270(B)	M

See also Coastal Ships

MOBELL MARINE DEVELOPMENT CO LTD

Havant

FUNNEL: Dark blue with black top.
HULL: Dark blue with red boot-topping.
AREA OF OPERATION: Portsmouth and South Coast contract work.

Name	Built	Tons Gross	Horse Power	Engines
Makikki ex Tanac	1944	55	270(B)	M

NEW MEDWAY STEAM PACKET CO LTD

Rochester

FUNNEL: None.
HULL: Dark grey.
AREA OF OPERATION: Rochester and River Medway.

Name	Built	Tons Gross	Horse Power	Engines
Acorn ex Hooligan-70	1934	32	105(B)	M

R. G. ODELL LTD

London

FUNNEL: Black with blue letter "O" on broad white band.
HULL: Black with two white lines and red boot-topping.
AREA OF OPERATION: River Thames (Lighterage).

Name	Built	Tons Gross	Horse Power	Engines
Churchill ex Denton-53, Mary Blake	1910	70	480(B)	M rbt fm SR

B. PERRY & SONS LTD

Bristol

FUNNEL: Yellow with black top.
HULL: Black with yellow topline.
AREA OF OPERATION: Bristol and Avonmouth (Lighterage).

Name	Built	Tons Gross	Horse Power	Engines
Salisbury ex B.P. 2-58, Tid 15	1943	45	350(B)	M rbt fm SR

PEVENSEY CASTLE LTD

Lowestoft

FUNNEL: Orange with houseflag.
HULL: Blue.

Name	Built	Tons Gross	Horse Power	Engines
Barkis ex Elmgarth-73	1960	75	400(B)	M

PORT OF LONDON AUTHORITY

London

FUNNEL: Yellow or Yellow with black top.
HULL: Black with red boot-topping.
AREA OF OPERATION: Ship towage in London enclosed docks; Dredging etc.; towage in River Thames.

Name	Built	Tons Gross	Horse Power	Engines
Dredging Fleet & *River Tugs:*				
Broodbank	1966	250	1,000(B)	M(2)/Pusher
Lord Devonport	1959	109	935(B)	M
Lord Waverley	1960	109	935(B)	M
Enclosed Dock Tugs:				
Lord Ritchie	1959	109	935(B)	M
Placard	1966	122	1,600(B)	M/VS
Plagal	1951	159	1,200(B)	M
Plangent	1951	159	1,200(B)	M
Plankton	1966	122	1,600(B)	M/VS
Plasma	1965	122	1,600(B)	M/VS
Platoon	1965	122	1,600(B)	M/VS

See also Harbour Works and Dredging Craft and Pilot Lighthouse and Buoy Tenders

PORT OF PRESTON AUTHORITY

Preston

FUNNEL: Black with Corporation armorial shield in pale blue and white.
HULL: Black with red boot-topping.
AREA OF OPERATION: Preston and River Ribble.

Name	Built	Tons Gross	Horse Power	Engines
Frank Jamieson	1956	146	720(B)	M(2)
Hewitt	1951	137	800(B)	M(2)
John Herbert	1955	146	720(B)	M(2)

See also Harbour Works and Dredging Craft

Top : VECTA, Southampton, Isle of Wight & South of England Royal Mail Steam Packet Co Ltd *F. R. Sherlock*

GENERAL VIII, Thames & General Lighterage Co Ltd *M. J. Gaston*

PORT OF SUNDERLAND AUTHORITY

Sunderland

FUNNEL: Yellow with black top and black sextant.
HULL: Black with white line and red boot-topping.
AREA OF OPERATION: Sunderland and River Wear.

Name	Built	Tons Gross	Horse Power	Engines
Pallion* ex Tid 72	1944	54	400(B)	M rbt fm SR

* Fitted with bow derrick
See also Harbour Works and Dredging Craft

PORT TALBOT DIVING & MARINE SERVICES CO LTD
(A. J. Doig)

Port Talbot

FUNNEL: Red with black top.
HULL: Black.
AREA OF OPERATION: Bristol Channel contract work.

Name	Built	Tons Gross	Horse Power	Engines
Tulagi ex Tanac	1946	54	200(B)	M

POUNDS SHIPOWNERS & SHIPBREAKERS LTD

Portsmouth

FUNNEL: Various markings.
HULL: Various colours.
AREA OF OPERATION: Portsmouth.

Name	Built	Tons Gross	Horse Power	Engines
Flying Wizard	1960	116	1,060(B)	M
Plaboy	1957	36	360(B)	M
Kitava ex Silvergilt-71, Esso Greenwich-66	1953	77	850(B)	M

REA TOWING CO LTD
(A subsidiary of Cory Ship Towage Ltd)

Birkenhead

FUNNEL: Red with black top separated by narrow white band and a white letter "R" on a white bordered black diamond.
HULL: Black with white line and red boot-topping.
AREA OF OPERATION: River Mersey and Coastal Towage.

Name	Built	Tons Gross	Horse Power	Engines
Beechgarth	1964	207	1,350(B)	M
Brackengarth	1969	334	3,380(B)	M/FF
Cedergarth	1962	213	1,300(B)	M
Foylegarth	1958	208	1,270(B)	M
ex Foylemore-69				
Hazelgarth	1959	230	1,680(B)	M
Hollygarth	1969	334	3,380(B)	M/FF
Kilgarth	1958	208	1,270(B)	M
ex Kilmore-69				
Maplegarth	1961	230	1,350(B)	M/FF
Willowgarth	1959	230	1,680(B)	M

See also Wm. Cory & Sons Ltd

J. ROBINSON

Rutherglen

FUNNEL: Yellow with deep black top.
HULL: Black with white line and red boot-topping.
AREA OF OPERATION:

Name	Built	Tons Gross	Horse Power	Engines
Duke of Normandy II	1934	54	295(B)	M
ex Duke of Normandy-72, Duke of Normandy II -50, F.K.O.1-49				

HARRY ROSE (TOWAGE) LTD

Poole

FUNNEL: Red with black top and white letters "HR" in white ring.
HULL: Black with white line and red boot-topping.
AREA OF OPERATION: Poole Harbour.

Name	Built	Tons Gross	Horse Power	Engines
Wendy Ann ex Vespa-74, Eveleen Brodstone	1934	92	600(B)	M
Wendy Ann 2	1940	44	500(B)	M

SATIM TOWAGE LTD

Ipswich

FUNNEL: Pale blue with broad white band.
HULL: Black.
AREA OF OPERATION: Rivers Stour and Orwell.

Name	Built	Tons Gross	Horse Power	Engines
Brett	1931	49	340(B)	M

S. B. TOWAGE LTD

Gravesend

FUNNEL: Blue with black top.
HULL: Black with red boot-topping.
AREA OF OPERATION: River Thames Contract work.

Name	Built	Tons Gross	Horse Power	Engines
Hembo	1953	80	560(B)	M
Presstan ex Pressman-73, Tyburn Brook-	1950	68	700(B)	M

SEAHAM HARBOUR DOCK CO LTD

Seaham

FUNNEL: Black with broad red band.
HULL: Black with red boot-topping.
AREA OF OPERATION: Seaham Harbour.

Name	Built	Tons Gross	Horse Power	Engines
Chipchase	1953	106	400(I)	SR(2)

SHIPBREAKING (QUEENBOROUGH) LTD

Cairnryan & Sheerness

FUNNEL:
HULL:
AREA OF OPERATION: Cairnryan and Medway.

Name	Built	Tons Gross	Horse Power	Engines
S.Q.L. 1 ex M.S.C. Nymph-70	1942	131	770(B)	M(2)
S.Q.L. 2 ex M.S.C. Neptune-70	1941	131	770(B)	M(2)

SHOREHAM PORT AUTHORITY

Brighton

FUNNEL: None.
HULL: Black.
AREA OF OPERATION: Shoreham.

Name	Built	Tons Gross	Horse Power	Engines
Kingston Buci	1960	76	650(B)	M

SOUTH OCEAN SERVICES LTD
(K. Ratcliff)

Portsmouth

FUNNEL: Dark blue with black top.
HULL: Blue with red boot-topping.
AREA OF OPERATION: Portsmouth or on contracts.

Name	Built	Tons Gross	Horse Power	Engines
Kendiken ex Wallasey-72	1954	200	950(I)	SR
Kokoda ex Silverclad-71, Esso Reading-66	1954	79	850(B)	M

SOUTHAMPTON, ISLE OF WIGHT & SOUTH OF ENGLAND ROYAL MAIL STEAM PACKET CO LTD

Southampton

FUNNEL: Red with black top with company symbol in red and white on superstructure.
HULL: Black with or without yellow line and red boot-topping.
AREA OF OPERATION: Southampton and the Solent; occasional Coastal Towage.

Name	Built	Tons Gross	Horse Power	Engines
Bonchurch ex Baie Comeau-66, Abeille No. 13, Tid 174	1944	54	360(B)	M rbt fm SR
Calshot	1964	494	1,800(B)	M(2)
Chale	1965	250	1,300(B)	M(2)
Culver	1956	246	1,340(B)	M(2)/K/FF
Dunnose	1958	241	1,340(B)	M(2)
Gatcombe	1970	269	2,500(B)	M/K/FF
Thorness	1961	247	1,340(B)	M(2)
Vecta	1970	269	2,500(B)	M/K/FF

See also Coastal Ships

SPILLER'S LTD

Hull

FUNNEL:
HULL:
AREA OF OPERATION: Hull and River Humber (Lighterage).

Name	Built	Tons Gross	Horse Power	Engines
Spiller's Rose	1954	39	250(B)	M

STATES OF JERSEY

Jersey, C.I.

FUNNEL: Yellow with black top separated by white band and States of Jersey armorial shield in white and red.
HULL: Black with white line and red boot-topping.
AREA OF OPERATION: Jersey.

Name	Built	Tons Gross	Horse Power	Engines
Duke of Normandy	1972	91	565(B)	M

STOUR SALVAGE LTD

Harwich

FUNNEL: Blue with white Maltese cross.
HULL: Black with red boot-topping.
AREA OF OPERATION: Harwich, Rivers Stour and Orwell.

Name	Built	Tons Gross	Horse Power	Engines
Rebel ex Flanchford-68	1921	58	320(B)	M
Rogue	19			M

M. & R. TALBOT

Folkestone

FUNNEL: Black with white letters "MR".
HULL: Black with red boot-topping.
AREA OF OPERATION: Contract work.

Name	Built	Tons Gross	Horse Power	Engines
Various ex Continental motor tugs (250-740 BHP)				

TEES & HARTLEPOOL PORT AUTHORITY

Middlesbrough

FUNNEL: Turquoise with gold company device and black top.
HULL: Black with red boot-topping.
AREA OF OPERATION: River Tees.

Name	Built	Tons Gross	Horse Power	Engines
Hart	1958	145	1,200(B)	M(2)
Seaton	1959	145	1,200(B)	M(2)
Stranton	1959	145	1,200(B)	M(2)
Wilton	1956	208	1,500(B)	M

See also Harbour Works and Dredging Craft section

TEES TOWING CO LTD

Middlesbrough

FUNNEL: Red with black top and two white bands.
HULL: Black with yellow line and red boot-topping.
AREA OF OPERATION: Middlesbrough and River Tees and Coastal and Short Sea Towage.

Name	Built	Tons Gross	Horse Power	Engines
Ayton Cross	1967	214	2,000(B)	M/K
Danby Cross	1961	114	750(B)	M/K
Erimus Cross	1960	192	1,200(B)	M
Fiery Cross	1957	192	1,200(B)	M/K/FF
Leven Cross	1971	141	1,250(B)	M/K/FF
Marton Cross	1963	133	1,100(B)	M
Ormesby Cross	1967	214	1,800(B)	M/K
Ralph Cross	1974	244	2,640(B)	M/K
New (2)	1974/5		2,200(B)	M/SCH(2)

THAMES & GENERAL LIGHTERAGE CO LTD

London

FUNNEL: Blue over red with narrow white top and large white letter "T" superimposed.
HULL: Black with white lines and orange boot-topping.
AREA OF OPERATION: River Thames (Lighterage).

Name	Built	Tons Gross	Horse Power	Engines
General VII	1962	63	665(B)	M
General VIII	1965	77	1,000(B)	M
Robertsbridge	1937	90	450(B)	M rbt fm SR

THAMES SERVICES (MARINE) LTD

Gravesend

FUNNEL: White with black top separated by broad blue band.
HULL: Black with red boot-topping.
AREA OF OPERATION: River Thames.

Name	Built	Tons Gross	Horse Power	Engines
Tern ex Stern-73				M
Turbulent ex Lash White-73, Lady Vera-69, Brahman-62	1938	208	910(B)	M rbt fm SR
Twizzle ex Mallard-73, M.S.C. Mallard-70	1939	129	840(B)	M(2)

See also Coastal Ship section

TRUSTEES OF THE HARBOUR OF DUNDEE

Dundee

FUNNEL: Yellow with narrow black top.
HULL: Black with yellow line and red boot-topping.

Name	Built	Tons Gross	Horse Power	Engines
Castlecraig ex Walcheren VIII-53	1951	139	660(B)	M
Harecraig II ex Flying Buzzard-6	1951	261	1,200(B)	M rbt fm SR

TYNE TUGS LTD

Newcastle

FUNNEL: Red with black top.
HULL: Black with red boot-topping.
AREA OF OPERATION: River Tyne and Coastal Towage. Tyne Tugs Ltd is the operating company for tugs owned by the two companies listed below.

Name	Built	Tons Gross	Horse Power	Engines
France, Fenwick Tyne & Wear Co Ltd:				
Alnmouth	1962	173	950(B)	M
Alnwick	1955	119	1,080(B)	M
Ashbrooke	1955	119	1,080(B)	M
Bamburgh	1956	119	1,080(B)	M
George V	1915	217	1,080(B)	M rbt fm SR
New	1974		3,180(B)	M
Lawson-Batey Tugs Ltd:				
Ironsider	1967	156	1,320(B)	M
Northsider	1967	156	1,320(B)	M
Quaysider	1955	137	1,200(B)	M
Roughsider	1958	143	750(B)	M
Westsider	1964	151	986(B)	M
New	1974		3,180(B)	M

UNITED TOWING (OCEAN TUGS) LTD
(United Towing (Tradesman) Ltd etc)
(Subsidiary of United Towing Ltd)

Hull

FUNNEL: White or pale yellow with black top with houseflag where possible (Houseflag: Blue swallowtail pennant with blue letter "U" superimposed on white star).
HULL: Black with white line and green boot-topping.
AREA OF OPERATION: Ocean Towage and Salvage, Coastal and Short-Sea Towage.

Name	Built	Tons Gross	Horse Power	Engines
Englishman	1965	574	4,250(B)	M(2)/SAL
Euroman	1967	1,182	5,340(B)	M/SAL
ex Bremen-72				
Irishman*	1967	451	5,000(B)	M(2)/SAL
Lloydsman	1971	2,041	16,000(B)	M/SAL
Masterman	1964	229	2,024(B)	M/SAL

* Operated by Star Offshore Services Ltd (United Towing Ltd/Blue Star Line)

Top: WELSHMAN, United Towing (Ocean Tugs) Ltd *'Fotoship'*

FOREMOST TROJAN, Westminster Dredging Co Ltd *M. J. Gaston*

United Towing (Ocean Tugs) Ltd (Continued)

Name	Built	Tons Gross	Horse Power	Engines
Norman* ex Jaramac 28-73, Frederic B. Ingram-72	1968	412	6,000(B)	M(2)/SAL
Scotsman* ex Jaramac 42-73, E. Bronson Ingram- 72	1969	412	6,000(B)	M(2)/SAL
Seaman	1967	261	2,400(B)	M(2)/SAL
Statesman I ex Statesman-73, Alice L. Moran-69	1966	1,167	12,000(B)	M(2)/SAL
Superman	1967	261	2,400(B)	M(2)/SAL
Tradesman	1964	230	2,024(B)	M(2)/SAL
Welshman*	1966	451	5,000(B)	M(2)/SAL

See also Humber Tugs Ltd

* *Operated by Star Offshore Services Ltd (United Towing Ltd/Blue Star Line)*

VOKINS & CO LTD

London

FUNNEL: Dark blue with red letter "V" on large white disc.
HULL: Black with white line and red boot-topping.
AREA OF OPERATION: River Thames (Lighterage).

Name	Built	Tons Gross	Horse Power	Engines
Vanoc	1937	58	390(B)	M
Vista	1940	71	420(B)	M
Voracious ex Gull	1929	64	500(B)	M rbt fm SR
Vortex ex Snowcem-64	1947	77	465(B)	M

S. W. WEEKS & CO LTD

Crayford, Essex

FUNNEL: Blue with blue "W" on white band.
HULL: Black.
AREA OF OPERATION: Plymouth and on Contract work.

Name	Built	Tons Gross	Horse Power	Engines
Louisa White	1949	39	300(B)	M

WELLAND RIVER CATCHMENT BOARD

Peterborough

FUNNEL: Yellow with black top.
HULL: Black.
AREA OF OPERATION: River Welland Area.

Name	Built	Tons Gross	Horse Power	Engines
W.D.B. Tug No. 3	1931	36	100(B) .	M

WESTMINSTER DREDGING CO LTD

London & Southampton

FUNNEL: Black with panel divided diagonally yellow over blue.
HULL: Black with grey topsides.
AREA OF OPERATION: Contract   work   with   Company   dredgers   and
hoppers throughout UK & Ireland.

Name	Built	Tons Gross	Horse Power	Engines
Beaver Crest	1966			M
Foremost Trojan	1968	72	495(B)	M
Jumsey	1928	30	180(B)	M rbt fm SR
Pullwell	1954	49	336(B)	M
Tideall ex Tid 43	1943	54	336(B)	M rbt fm SR
Tiderip ex Tideway-72, Tid 120	1945	54	336(B)	M rbt fm SR

See also Harbour Works and Dredging Craft

JOHN H. WHITAKER (HOLDINGS) LTD

Hull

FUNNEL: Black with white letter "W" superimposed on narrow red over black over narrow green bands.
HULL: Black.
AREA OF OPERATION: Hull and River Humber.

Name	Built	Tons Gross	Horse Power	Engines
Wilberforce	1920	45	250(B)	M rbt fm SR

See also Coastal Ships

A. WHITE

London

FUNNEL: Black with white letter "W".
HULL: Black with white line and red boot-topping.
AREA OF OPERATION: River Thames (Lighterage).

Name	Built	Tons Gross	Horse Power	Engines
Boys White ex Rodney II-68	1934	38	350(B)	M
Doris White ex Prima	1930	40	400(B)	M
Knocker White ex Cairnrock	1924	96	350(B)	M rbt fm SR
John White ex Irande-73	1929	96	350(B)	M rbt fm SR

TiLBuRy
2·10·81

Also the smaller tug Algonda

R. K. WOOD

Newhaven

FUNNEL: Black with company device incorporating letter "W" in white.
HULL: Black with red boot-topping.
AREA OF OPERATION: English Channel and Coastal towage.

Name	Built	Tons Gross	Horse Power	Engines
Chelsea ex Meads-58	1940	67	500(B)	M rbt fm SR

R. K. Wood (Continued)

Name	Built	Tons Gross	Horse Power	Engines
Ocean Puller ex River Orwell-72, Topmast No. 9-49, Lumme-48	1943	145	900(B)	M

WILLIAMS SHIPPING CO (FAWLEY) LTD

Southampton

FUNNEL: Black with houseflag on orange band (Houseflag: Divided diagonally orange over blue with blue letters "WS" on black diamond.)
HULL: Black with orange line and red boot-topping separated by white line.
AREA OF OPERATION: Southampton and The Solent (Lighterage) and Contract/Diving work in the area.

Name	Built	Tons Gross	Horse Power	Engines
Willanne	1932	38	204(B)	M

See also Coastal Ships

WIMPEY (MARINE) LTD

London

FUNNEL: Brown with black top.
HULL: Black with red boot-topping.
AREA OF OPERATION: Contract Work.

Name	Built	Tons Gross	Horse Power	Engines
G.W. 180 ex Tregarth-70, Neylandia-61	1958	102	500(B)	M
G.W. 196	1974	90		M

WOODFORDS (LONDON) LTD

Twickenham

FUNNEL: Yellow.
HULL: Yellow.
AREA OF OPERATION: Southampton, The Solent and Langstone Harbour.

Name	Built	Tons Gross	Horse Power	Engines
Bess ex Industrious-73 (65), Tanac. -66	1944	55	240(B)	M

See also Coastal Ships

WORKINGTON DOCK & HARBOUR BOARD

Workington

FUNNEL: Black with broad white band.
HULL: Black with red boot-topping.
AREA OF OPERATION: Workington.

Name	Built	Tons Gross	Horse Power	Engines
Solway ex Empire Ann-48	1943	232	900(I)	SR

DUBLIN PORT AND DOCKS BOARD

Dublin

FUNNEL: Yellow with black top.
HULL: Black with white line and red boot-topping separated by white line.
AREA OF OPERATION: Dublin and River Liffey.

Name	Built	Tons Gross	Horse Power	Engines
Ben Eader	1972	198	1,600(B)	M/VS(2)
Coliemore ex Applesider-72	1962	173	1,000(B)	M
Cluain Tarbh	1963	178	1,268(B)	M/FF

CORK HARBOUR COMMISSIONERS

Cork

FUNNEL: White with black top.
HULL: Black with white line and red boot-topping.
AREA OF OPERATION: Cork.

Name	Built	Tons Gross	Horse Power	Engines
Richard Wallace ex Zed, Tid 108	1944	54	220(I)	SR
Shandon ex Flying Dolphin-68	1959	109	1,000(B)	M

A.C. CRANES

Dublin

FUNNEL: Pale blue with black top.
HULL: Black with red boot-topping.
AREA OF OPERATION: Coastal towage and contract work.

Name	Built	Tons Gross	Horse Power	Engines
Dunheron ex Golden Cross-68	1955	132	882(B)	M

HAULBOWLINE INDUSTRIES LTD

Cork

FUNNEL: Yellow with black top.
HULL: Black with white line and red boot-topping.
AREA OF OPERATION: Cork and Contract/Diving work in area.

Name	Built	Tons Gross	Horse Power	Engines
Landy II	1949	66	204(B)	M(2)

HENRY & CO LTD

Waterford

FUNNEL:
HULL:
AREA OF OPERATION: Waterford and River Suir.

Name	Built	Tons Gross	Horse Power	Engines
Gnat	1934	66	390(B)	M

TRAWLERS

ABUNDA FISHING CO LTD

Grimsby

FUNNEL: Blue with gold trident and black top.
HULL: Black with red boot-topping.

Name	Port Registry	Date	Gross Tons	Engines
Belgaum	GY.218	1956	577	M

DEPT. OF AGRICULTURE & FISHERIES FOR SCOTLAND

Edinburgh

FUNNEL: Yellow with black top.
HULL: Black with white line and red boot-topping.

Name	Port Registry	Date	Gross Tons	Engines
Fishery Research Trawler:				
Scotia	No Fishing Number	1971	1,521	DE(A)

Top: BELGAUM, Abunda Fishing Co Ltd *T. J. M. Wood*

BOSTON BLENHEIM, Boston Deep Sea Fisheries Ltd *J. Clarkson*

ALBERT FISHING CO LTD

Hartlepool

FUNNEL: Red with black top and red pennant houseflag.
HULL: Black with red boot-topping.

Name	Port Registry	Date	Gross Tons	Engines
Cleveland ex Boston Valiant-72, Valiant Star-72	HL.93	1959	160	M

ALFRED BANNISTER (TRAWLERS) LTD

Grimsby

FUNNEL: Black with houseflag.
HULL: Black with red boot-topping.

Name	Port Registry	Date	Gross Tons	Engines
Saxon Forward	GY.688	1962	204	M
Saxon Onward	GY.618	1960	210	M
Forward Steam Fishing Co Ltd:				
Saxon Progress	GY.655	1961	197	M
Alfred Bannister (Trawlers) Ltd & Forward Steam Fishing Co Ltd:				
Saxon Venture	GY.616	1959	211	M
Saxon Trawlers Ltd:				
Saxon Ranger* ex Atlantic Seal-65	GY.1396	1961	286	M

* Stern Trawler

GEORGE A. BECK

Kendal

FUNNEL:
HULL:

Name	Port Registry	Date	Gross Tons	Engines
Faithlie	A.100	1957	169	M

BICKLEY FISHING CO LTD

Aberdeen

FUNNEL:
HULL:

Name	Port Registry	Date	Gross Tons	Engines
Bickleigh	LT.444	1962	164	M

BOSTON DEEP SEA FISHERIES LTD

Fleetwood, Grimsby, Hull & Lowestoft

FUNNEL: Red with or without black top.
HULL: Black with white line and red boot-topping.

Name	Port Registry	Date	Gross Tons	Engines
Boston Argosy	LT.364	1960	195	M
Boston Beverley*	GY.191	1971	517	M
Boston Blenheim*	FD.137	1971	517	M
Boston Boeing	GY.183	1962	707	M
Boston Comanche ex Saint Louis-68	GY.144	1959	616	M
Boston Comet†	LT.183	1960	137	M
Boston Concord	GY.730	1965	758	M
Boston Coronet	LT.459	1959	199	M
Boston Explorer ex Aberdeen Explorer-68	FD.15	1965	425	M
Boston Hornet	LT.173	1960	131	M
Boston Lightning ex Admiral Burnett-68	FD.14	1961	391	M

* Stern Trawler   † Oil rig safety duty

Boston Deep Sea Fisheries Ltd (Continued)

Name	Port Registry	Date	Gross Tons	Engines
Boston Lincoln*	GY.1399	1968	994	M
Boston Phantom	FD.252	1965	431	M
Boston Sea Dart*	LT.94	1972	312	M
Boston Sea Fury*	LT.139	1972	312	M
Boston Sea Sprite*	LT.247	1972	311	M
Boston Wasp	LT.238	1960	300	M
Princess Ann*	H.	1974	1476	M
D. B. Finn	H.332	1961	701	M
Lady Parkes*	H.397	1966	1,033	M
St. Chad	H.20	1956	575	M
Sir Fred Parkes*	H.385	1966	1,033	M
Brixham Trawlers Ltd:				
Boston Nimrod	LT. 49	1956	315	M
Boston Seafire	FD.109	1956	314	M
ex Buzzard-61				
Carry On Fishing Co Ltd:				
Boston Corsair	LT.148	1959	135	M
Fleetwood Near Water Trawlers Ltd:				
Boston Viscount	LT.509	1965	174	M
Grimsby Near Water Trawlers Ltd:				
Boston Shackleton	LT.714	1960	310	M
ex Haselbeach-65				
Iago Steam Trawler Co Ltd:				
Boston Attacker	FD.169	1959	448	M
ex Captain Fremantle-72				
Boston Crusader	FD.208	1958	402	M
ex Broadwater-72				
Boston Defender	FD.163	1957	391	M
ex Captain Riou-72				
Boston Invader	FD.161	1955	407	M
ex Red Rose-72				
Boston Marauder	FD.168	1958	444	M
ex Captain Hardy-72				
Boston Tristar	GY.210	1960	434	M
ex Captain Foley-72				
Looker Fishing Co Ltd:				
Boston Beaver	LT.445	1962	165	M

* Stern Trawler

Boston Deep Sea Fisheries Ltd (Continued)

Name	Port Registry	Date	Gross Tons	Engines
Parbel-Smith Ltd:				
Prince Philip	GY.138	1963	442	M
William Wilberforce	GY.140	1959	698	M
Basil A. Parkes & Others:				
Boston Kestrel	FD.256	1966	431	N
Robin Trawler Ltd:				
Boston Provost	LT.274	1960	200	M
Prince Charles	H.77	1958	691	M
F. & T. Ross Ltd:				
Boston Whirlwind	LT.454	1962	165	M
St. Andrew's Steam Fishing Co Ltd:				
Boston Wayfarer	LT.508	1965	174	M

* *Stern Trawler*
† *Oil rig safety device*
See also Tugs

BOYD LINE LTD

Hull

FUNNEL: White with black top and two red bands.
HULL: Black with red line and red boot-topping.

Name	Port Registry	Date	Gross Tons	Engines
Arctic Avenger ex Ross Columbia-67, Cape Columbia-66	H.118	1956	806	SR
Arctic Brigand ex Marbella-65	H.52	1955	793	SR
Arctic Buccaneer*	H.188	1973	1,600	M
Arctic Cavalier	H.204	1960	764	M

* *Stern Trawler*

Boyd Line Ltd (Continued)

Name	Port Registry	Date	Gross Tons	Engines
Arctic Corsair	H.320	1960	764	M
Arctic Freebooter*	H.362	1966	1,183	M
Arctic Galliard*	H.195	1973	1,580	M
Arctic Privateer*†	H.441	1968	928	M
Arctic Raider*	H.440	1968	928	M
Arctic Ranger	H.155	1957	867	SR
Arctic Vandal	H.344	1961	594	M
Arctic Warrior	H.176	1951	712	SR
Wm. Liston Ltd, Edinburgh:				
Arctic Attacker ex Kirmington-73, Admiral Cunningham-65, Star of Scotland-63	GY.1367	1960	226	M
Arctic Crusader ex Summervale-73	LH.373	1960	217	M
Arctic Explorer ex Barbara Paton-72	GW.7	1957	273	M
Arctic Hunter ex Gregor Paton-72	GW.9	1958	273	M
Arctic Invader ex Admiral Rodney-72, Star of Aberdeen-63	A.199	1958	249	M
Arctic Scout ex Kelso Paton-72	GW.2	1956	274	M
Arctic Viking ex Syerston-73, Admiral Ramsey-65, Star of the Isles-63	GY.1366	1960	226	M
New (2)	GN.	1974/75		M

* Stern Trawler
† Owned by Ministry of Agriculture Fisheries & Food; converting to Weather/Mother ship

BRITISH UNITED TRAWLERS LTD
Hull & Grimsby

FUNNEL: Blue with black top and blue letters "BUT" between wavy blue lines on white band.
HULL: Black or blue with red boot-topping.

Name	Port Registry	Date	Gross Tons	Engines
British United Trawlers Finance Ltd:				
Dane*	H.144	1973	1,480	M(A)

* Stern Trawler

Top: CONQUEROR, Northern Trawlers Ltd *T. J. M. Wood*

EREDENE, Beaconhill Fishing Co Ltd *T. J. M. Wood*

British United Trawlers Ltd (Continued)

Name	Port Registry	Date	Gross Tons	Engines
Goth*	GY.252	1973	1,450	M(A)
Norse*	H.193	1973	1,300	M(A)
Pict*	H.150	1973	1,478	M(A)
Roman*	GY.253	1973	1,488	M(A)
Goweroak Ltd, Grimsby:				
Ross Cheetah	GY.614	1959	354	M
Ross Civet	GY.652	1960	352	M
Ross Cougar	GY.531	1958	355	M
Ross Eagle	GY.656	1961	288	M
Ross Falcon	GY.667	1961	288	M
Ross Genet	GY.650	1960	352	M
Ross Hawk	GY.657	1961	288	M
Ross Jackal	GY.637	1959	355	M
Ross Jaguar	GY.494	1957	355	M
Ross Juno ex Padgett-65	GY.660	1961	413	M
Ross Kandahar ex Kandahar-62	GY.123	1958	507	M
Ross Kashmir	GY.122	1957	489	M
Ross Kelly ex Kelly-62	GY.125	1956	469	M
Ross Kelvin ex Kelvin-62	GY.60	1958	468	M
Ross Kestrel	GY.658	1961	288	M
Ross Khartoum ex Khartoum-62	GY.120	1958	507	M
Ross Kipling ex Kipling-62	GY.126	1957	469	M
Ross Kittiwake	GY.678	1961	288	M
Ross Leopard	GY.491	1957	355	M
Ross Lynx	GY.626	1960	354	M
Ross Panther	GY.519	1958	355	M
Ross Tiger	GY.398	1957	355	M
Ross Zebra	GY.653	1960	352	M
Northern Trawlers Ltd, Grimsby:				
Black Watch	GY.23	1956	697	SR
Coldstreamer	GY.10	1955	697	SR
Conqueror*	GY.1364	1965	1,157	M
Defiance*	GY.1377	1966	1,113	M
Lord Beatty	GY.91	1956	697	SR
Lord Mountevans	GY.79	1951	712	SR
Northern Chief	GY.128	1950	692	SR
Northern Eagle	GY.22	1956	701	SR
Northern Isles	GY.149	1950	692	SR
Northern Jewel	GY.1	1954	799	SR
Northern Prince	GY.121	1949	677	SR
Northern Queen	GY.124	1949	677	SR
Northern Sceptre	GY.297	1954	804	SR
Northern Sea	GY.142	1950	692	SR

* Stern Trawler

British United Trawlers Ltd (Continued)

Name	Port Registry	Date	Gross Tons	Engines
Northern Sky ex Ross Repulse-68, Statham-65	GY.25	1956	701	SRT
Northern Sun ex Wyre Mariner-68	GY.2	1956	657	SR
Ross Intrepid* ex Ross Kennedy-66, Cape Kennedy-66	H.353	1965	804	DE
Ross Valiant*	GY.729	1964	803	DE
Royal Lincs	GY.18	1955	697	SRT
Vanessa	GY.257	1952	661	SR
Velinda	GY.29	1956	779	SR
Ross Trawlers Ltd, *Grimsby:*				
Lord Jellicoe	GY.709	1962	594	M
Northern Gift	GY.704	1962	576	M
Northern Reward	GY.694	1962	576	M
Ross Ramillies ex Ross Fighter-66, Andanes-61	GY.53	1950	673	M
Ross Renown	GY.666	1962	790	M
Ross Revenge ex Freyr-63	GY.718	1960	978	M
Ross Rodney ex Rodney-62	GY.34	1957	697	M
Ross Vanguard*	GY.1372	1966	1,060	M
Vianova	GY.590	1959	559	M
Vivaria	GY.648	1960	744	M
G. F. Sleight & Son Ltd, Hull:				
Locarno ex Longest-65	GY.303	1959	324	M

* Stern Trawler

BRITISH UNITED TRAWLERS (ABERDEEN) LTD

Aberdeen

FUNNEL & HULL: Various colours and markings.

Name	Port Registry	Date	Gross Tons	Engines
North Eastern Fisheries *Ltd:*				
Mount Eden	A.152	1957	293	M

British United Trawlers (Aberdeen) Ltd (Continued)

Name	Port Registry	Date	Gross Tons	Engines
Seafield Fishing Co Ltd:				
Mount Everest	A.42	1955	303	M
Mount Sorrell	A.634	1963	212	M
Stroud's Steam Fishing Co Ltd:				
Mount Melleray	A.558	1961	216	M
Spey Motor Trawlers Ltd:				
Speyside	A.4	1958	328	M

BRITISH UNITED TRAWLERS (GRANTON) LTD

Granton

FUNNEL: Blue with black letters "BUT" between wavy blue lines on white band.
HULL: Blue with white line and red boot-topping.

Name	Port Registry	Date	Gross Tons	Engines
Granton Falcon	GN.16	1956	272	M
Granton Harrier	GN.77	1962	212	M
Granton Merlin	GN.72	1960	235	M
Granton Osprey	GN.19	1960	230	M
Joe Croan	LH.73	1956	273	M
Malcolm Croan	A.444	1960	234	M
Maureen Croan	A.434	1960	234	M
Ross Mallard	GY.699	1962	266	M
Goweroak Ltd:				
Ross Cormorant	GY.665	1961	288	M
Ross Curlew	GY.692	1962	288	M
Ross Heron	GY.693	1961	288	M

BRITISH UNITED TRAWLERS (HULL) LTD

Hull

FUNNEL: Blue with black letters "BUT" between wavy blue lines on white band.
HULL: Blue with red boot-topping.

Name	Port Registry	Date	Gross Tons	Engines
Afghan* ex Ranger Boreas-73 Blankenese-70	H.237	1965	928	M
Arab* ex Ranger Cadmus-73	H.238	1971	1,106	M
Esquimaux* ex Ranger Aurora-73	H.236	1966	779	M
Hausa† ex Ranger Briseis-73, Fritz Homann-70	No Fishing Number	1962	982	M
Kelt* ex Ranger Calliope-73	H.240	1972	1,106	M
Kurd* ex Ranger Callisto-73	H.242	1972	1,106	M
Turcoman* ex Ranger Apollo-73	H.233	1965	778	M

* *Stern Freezer Trawlers*

† *Converted Weather/Mother Ship duties*

BRUCEWOOD (ABERDEEN) LTD

Aberdeen

FUNNEL & HULL: Various markings and colours.

Name	Port Registry	Date	Gross Tons	Engines
Beaconhill Fishing Co Ltd:				
Eredene	A.554	1961	217	M
Bruce's Stores (Aberdeen) Ltd:				
Admiral Hawke	A.520	1961	225	M

Brucewood (Aberdeen) Ltd (Continued)

Name	Port Registry	Date	Gross Tons	Engines
Bruce's Stores (Aberdeen) & Others:				
Cromdale	A.365	1969	119	M
Salamis	A.	1974	120	M
Seaward Quest	A.289	1959	214	M
Spinningdale	A.473	1968	103	M
W. M. Ellen & Others:				
Seaward Petrel	A.412	1959	214	M
S. G. Farquhar & Others:				
Glenelg	A.696	1972	117	M

PHILIP BUCHAN & JOSEPH BUCHAN JNR.

Peterhead

FUNNEL:
HULL:

Name	Port Registry	Date	Gross Tons	Engines
Viking Deeps ex George Craig-73, launched as John Watterston	PD.75	1957	197	M

JAMES D. CARSON & OTHERS

Anstruther

FUNNEL:
HULL:

Name	Port Registry	Date	Gross Tons	Engines
Spes Aurea	KY.377	1953	115	M

THE CEVIC STEAM FISHING CO LTD

Fleetwood

FUNNEL: Black with two red bands.
HULL: Black with red boot-topping.

Name	Port Registry	Date	Gross Tons	Engines
Arlanda	FD.206	1961	431	M

JAMES R. CHEESEMAN

Burgh Castle, Suffolk

FUNNEL: Dark blue with black top.
HULL: Black with red boot-topping.

Name	Port Registry	Date	Gross Tons	Engines
Wilson Line	YH.105	1932	128	M

G. D. CLARIDGE

Lowestoft

FUNNEL: Blue with houseflag (White with blue letter "C") and black top.
HULL: Black or grey with white line and red boot-topping.

Name	Port Registry	Date	Gross Tons	Engines
Claridge Trawlers Ltd:				
Anguilla	LT.67	1959	228	M
Barbados	LT.312	1958	213	M
Bermuda	LT.122	1955	205	M
British Honduras	LT.134	1937	147	M

G. D. Claridge (Continued)

Name	Port Registry	Date	Gross Tons	Engines
Cuttlefish	LT.65	1959	153	M
Kingfish	LT.186	1955	151	M
Loch Laoi	LT.332	1949	109	M
Loch Lorgan	LT.335	1949	106	M
St. David	LT.494	1947	335	M
ex Allan Water-65				
St. Georges	LT.402	1946	343	M
ex Thorina-65				
St. John	LT.7	1969	241	M
St. Kitts	LT.481	1941	316	M
ex Postboy-65,				
Milford Marquis-51				
St. Nicola	LT.83	1949	349	M
ex Joli Fructidor-69,				
Milford Duchess-54				
St. Rose	LT.82	1949	349	M
ex Jean Vacquelin-				
68, Milford Duke				
St. Thomas	LT.8	1969	241	M
Spearfish	LT.232	1956	151	M

Clan Steam Fishing Co (Grimsby) Ltd:

Trinidad	LT.210	1950	168	M
ex Milford Knight-55				

Colne Fishing Co Ltd:

Antigua	LT.150	1957	204	M
Bahama	LT.142	1957	204	M
St.Martin	LT.376	1961	254	M

Dragon Fishing Co Ltd:

Grenada	LT.130	1955	205	M
Jamaica	LT.185	1947	285	M
ex Star of				
Scotland-60				
St. Lucia	LT.362	1961	254	M
Sawfish	LT.66	1959	153	M
New (2)	LT.	1975		M

Drifter Trawlers Ltd:

Anglerfish	LT.391	1961	153	M
Dominica	LT.314	1958	213	M
Una	LT.198	1950	114	M

Huxley Fishing Co Ltd:

Montserrat	LT.64	1959	228	M
Rockfish	LT.244	1956	151	M
Silverfish	LT.340	1961	160	M

Top: ST. NICOLA, Claridge Trawlers Ltd *B. G. Banham*

CARLISLE, Rhondda Fishing Co Ltd *T. J. M. Wood*

CONSOLIDATED FISHERIES LTD
(Sir John R. Marsden Bart.)

Grimsby

FUNNEL: Yellow with red crown on broad white band separating grey from black top.
HULL: Black with blue line and red boot-topping.

Name	Port Registry	Date	Gross Tons	Engines
Arsenal	GY.48	1958	744	SR
Everton	GY.58	1958	884	SR
Grimsby Town	GY.246	1953	711	SR
Hull City	GY.282	1953	711	SR
Rhondda Fishing Co Ltd:				
Barnsley	GY.651	1960	441	M
Carlisle	GY.681	1961	441	M
Crystal Palace	GY.683	1962	441	M
Notts Forest	GY.649	1960	441	M
Real Madrid	GY.674	1961	441	M
Wendover Fishing Co (Grimsby) Ltd:				
Aldershot	GY.612	1959	427	M
Blackburn Rovers	GY.706	1962	439	M
Gillingham	GY.622	1960	427	M
Huddersfield Town	GY.702	1962	439	M
Port Vale	GY.484	1957	427	M
Spurs	GY.697	1962	439	M

GEORGE CRAIG & SONS LTD

Aberdeen

FUNNEL: Grey with black top separated by narrow red over white bands.
HULL: Black with white line and red boot-topping.

Name	Port Registry	Date	Gross Tons	Engines
Admiral Frobisher	A.159	1957	274	M
Cevic	FD.241	1958	249	M
Coastal Empress	A.455	1960	250	M
Grampian Crest	A.393	1960	211	M
Grampian Glen	A.518	1961	214	M
Grampian Heather	A.436	1973	120	M
Grampian Hill	A.517	1960	214	M
Grampian Monarch*	A.337	1973	480	M
Mary Craig	A.263	1959	197	M

* Stern Trawler

George Craig & Sons Ltd (Continued)

Name	Port Registry	Date	Gross Tons	Engines
Scottish King	A.378	1959	280	M
Scottish Princess	A.382	1959	280	M
Scottish Queen	A.210	1958	278	M
H. K. F. Trawlers Ltd:				
Admiral Drake	A.514	1960	306	M
Admiral Jellicoe	A.515	1961	306	M
Boston Hercules	A.160	1960	310	M
George Craig & Sons Ltd & John L. Bowman:				
Grampian Eagle	A.355	1973	114	M
John S. Bowman & Others:				
Grampian Cairn	A.346	1973	114	M

* *Stern Trawler*

CRAIG STORES (ABERDEEN) LTD
(British United Trawlers Group)

Aberdeen

FUNNEL: Blue with black letters "BUT" between wavy blue lines on white band.
HULL: Blue with or without white line and red boot-topping.

Name	Port Registry	Date	Gross Tons	Engines
Ardenlea ex Jarishof-66	A.805	1963	206	M
Ashlea ex Welsh Princess-67	A.841	1963	308	M
Birchlea ex Ross Badger-68, Welsh Consort-67	A.58	1962	308	M
Cederlea ex Ross Beaver-68, Welsh Monarch-67	A.67	1962	308	M
Rowanlea ex Welsh Prince-67	A.832	1963	308	M
Summerlee	A.577	1956	274	M
Southburn (Fishing) Ltd:				
Lindenlea	A.409	1960	281	M

D. A. M. ENGINEERS LTD
Plymouth

FUNNEL: Yellow with white letters "DAM" on black top.
HULL: Black.

Name	Port Registry	Date	Gross Tons	Engines
Vigilance	A.204	1958	149	M

Also smaller trawlers under 100 grt

T. DAVIDSON
Aberdeen

FUNNEL: Various markings.
HULL: Various colours.

Name	Port Registry	Date	Gross Tons	Engines
Craigwood Ltd:				
Admiral Mountbatten	A.186	1958	258	M
Lothian Trawling Co Ltd:				
Burnbanks ex Lothian Leader-72	A.163	1959	215	M
W. G. Wilson Port Knockie:				
W. R. Deeside	A.374	1972	107	M

DEVANHA FISHING CO LTD
Aberdeen

FUNNEL: Red with white flying seagul interlocking large black letter "D" and black top.
HULL: Black with red boot-topping.

Name	Port Registry	Date	Gross Tons	Engines
Carency	A.573	1961	209	M
Gilmar	A.468	1960	215	M
Kinellan	A.578	1961	209	M

DIAMONDS STEAM FISHING CO LTD

Grimsby

FUNNEL: Three white diamonds on broad red band between two narrow blue bands separating yellow from black top.
HULL: Black with white topline and red boot-topping.

Name	Port Registry	Date	Gross Tons	Engines
Erimo	GY.691	1962	273	M
Osako	GY.600	1958	325	M
Tokio	GY.661	1961	273	M
Japan Fishing Co Ltd:				
Okino	GY.689	1962	273	M
Yesso	GY.610	1958	325	M
Taylor Steam Fishing Co Ltd:				
Hondo	GY.668	1961	273	M
Ogano	GY.608	1959	320	M

C. V. EASTICK LTD

Gt. Yarmouth

FUNNEL: Black with houseflag.
HULL: Black.

Name	Port Registry	Date	Gross Tons	Engines
Brave Buccaneer ex Boston Buccaneer-73	LT.157	1961	165	M
Hawkflight	A.215	1961	174	M

STANLEY GOOCH

Newhaven

FUNNEL:
HULL:

Name	Port Registry	Date	Gross Tons	Engines
Yellowtail	LT.326	1945	119	M

GOWAN FISHING CO LTD
Aberdeen

FUNNEL: Yellow with black top separated by silver over blue bands.
HULL: Green with red boot-topping.

Name	Port Registry	Date	Gross Tons	Engines
Craig-Gowan	A.323	1960	163	M

THOMAS HAMLING & CO LTD
Hull

FUNNEL: Yellow with black top separated by broad red band.
HULL: Black with red boot-topping.

Name	Port Registry	Date	Gross Tons	Engines
St. Benedict*	H.164	1972	1,550	M
St. Britwin	H.124	1950	742	SR
St. Dominic	H.116	1958	829	DE
St. Gerontius	H.350	1962	659	M
St. Giles	H.220	1962	658	M
St. Jason*	H.436	1967	1,288	M
St. Jasper*	H.31	1969	1,286	M
St. Jerome*	H.442	1968	1,288	M
St. Keverne	H.15	1951	746	SR
St. Leger	H.178	1951	746	SR
Firth Steam Trawling Co Ltd:				
St. Apollo	H.592	1948	658	SR

* *Stern Trawlers*

HELLYER BROS. LTD
(British United Trawlers Ltd)
Hull

FUNNEL: Yellow, with or without black top, with or without houseflag (White "H" on blue).
HULL: Grey with white line and red boot-topping. (Some vessels operating in "BUT" colours.)

Name	Port Registry	Date	Gross Tons	Engines
Benvolio	H.22	1949	722	SR

Top: GRAMPIAN CREST, George Craig & Sons Ltd *T. J. M. Wood*

INVINCIBLE, Hudson Brothers Trawlers Ltd *T. J. M. Wood*

Hellyer Bros. Ltd (Continued)

Name	Port Registry	Date	Gross Tons	Engines
Falstaff	H.107	1959	896	DE
Kingston Almandine	H.104	1950	725	SR
ex St. Hubert-51				
Kingston Amber	H.326	1960	785	M
Kingston Beryl	H.128	1959	691	M
Kingston Emerald	H.49	1954	811	SR
Kingston Jacinth	H.198	1952	794	SR
Kingston Jade	H.149	1951	794	SR
Kingston Onyx	H.140	1950	794	SR
Kingston Pearl	H.127	1958	691	M
Kingston Sapphire	H.95	1955	809	SR
Kingston Topaz	H.145	1950	794	SR
Loch Eriboll	H.323	1960	734	M
Lord Alexander	H.12	1954	790	SR
Lord Lovat	H.148	1951	713	SR
Lord Nelson*	H.330	1961	904	M
Lord St. Vincent	H.261	1962	594	M
Lord Tedder	H.154	1951	722	SR
Lorenzo	H.230	1952	830	SR
Macbeth	H.201	1957	810	SR
ex St. Matthew-69,				
Breughel-61				
Newby Wyke	H.111	1950	672	SR
Portia	H.24	1956	883	DE
Ross Implacable*	H.6	1968	1,042	M
Ross Resolution	GY.527	1948	564	M
Hudson Brothers				
Trawlers Ltd:				
Invincible*	H.96	1970	1,085	M
Ross Altair	H.279	1963	677	M
ex Stella Altair-65				
Ross Aquila	H.114	1956	780	M
ex Stella Aquila-65				
Ross Canaveral	H.267	1963	805	M
ex Cape Canaveral-				
66				
Ross Illustrious*	H.419	1966	1,076	M
Ross Leonis	H.322	1960	775	M
ex Stella Leonis-65				
Ross Orion	H.235	1962	778	M
ex Stella Orion-66				
Ross Otranto	H.227	1962	823	M
ex Cape Otranto-66				
Ross Sirius	H.277	1963	677	M
ex Stella Sirius-65				
Ross Trafalgar	H.59	1957	787	DE
ex Cape Trafalgar-66				
Wilemace Ltd:				
Cassio*	H.398	1966	1574	M
Coriolanus*	H.412	1967	1105	M

* Stern Trawler

Hellyer Bros Ltd (Continued)

Name	Port Registry	Date	Gross Tons	Engines
Orsino†	H.410	1966	1,131	M
Othello*	H.581	1966	1,113	M

* *Stern Trawler*
† *Converted Weather/Mother Ship duties*

HEWARD TRAWLERS LTD

London & Fleetwood

FUNNEL: Black with blue houseflag.
HULL: Grey with blue line and red boot-topping.

Name	Port Registry	Date	Gross Tons	Engines
Ella Hewett	LO.94	1964	567	M
Kennedy	FD.139	1957	426	M
ex Boston				
Britannia-69				
Robert Hewett	LO.65	1961	567	M
Ssafa	FD.155	1958	416	M
The Hewett Fishing				
Co Ltd:				
London Town	LO.70	1960	228	M
Royalist	LO.50	1960	228	M

HERD & MACKENZIE & OTHERS

Buckie

FUNNEL:
HULL:

Name	Port Registry	Date	Gross Tons	Engines
Loch Kildonan	PD.79	1956	149	M

HOBSON'S (LOWESTOFT) LTD

Lowestoft

FUNNEL: Orange with or without black top and houseflag.
HULL: Grey with red boot-topping or black.

Name	Port Registry	Date	Gross Tons	Engines
A. J. Buchan & Others, Fraserburgh:				
Golden Promise	FR.186	1957	134	M
Small & Co (Lowestoft) Ltd:				
Constance Banks	LT.979	1967	255	M
Roy Stevens	LT.271	1961	202	M
Suffolk Challenger	LT.555	1968	255	M
Suffolk Chieftain	LT.556	1968	255	M
Suffolk Conquest*	LT.317	1973	390	M
Suffolk Craftsman	LT.422	1961	202	M
Suffolk Crusader	LT.557	1968	255	M
Suffolk Endeavour ex Imprevu-65, Boston Vanguard-62	LT.789	1968	255	M
Suffolk Enterprise	LT.492	1957	245	M
Suffolk Harvester*	LT.175	1972	380	M
Suffolk Kinsman	LT.397	1960	202	M
Suffolk Mariner	LT.378	1961	202	M
Suffolk Monarch*	LT.170	1973	392	M
Suffolk Punch	LT.395	1961	202	M
Suffolk Venture	LT.777	1967	255	M
Suffolk Warrior*	LT.171	1973	392	M

* *Stern Trawler*

RICHARD IRVIN & SONS LTD

Aberdeen & N. Shields

FUNNEL: Black with two red bands.
HULL: Black with red boot-topping.

Name	Port Registry	Date	Gross Tons	Engines
Ben Asdale*	A.328	1972	442	M
Ben Bhrackie	A.814	1966	443	M
Ben Chourn	SN.20	1960	278	M
Ben Edra*	SN.	1974	370	M
Ben Gairn	A.508	1961	373	M
Ben Glas	SN.41	1961	219	M
Ben Gulvain	A.751	1965	443	M
Ben Heilem	A.553	1961	372	M

* *Stern Trawler*

Top: CONSTANCE BANKS, Small & Co (Lowestoft) Ltd *B. G. Banham*

TOM GRANT, Lindsey Trawlers Ltd *T. J. M. Wood*

Richard Irvin & Sons Ltd (Continued)

Name	Port Registry	Date	Gross Tons	Engines
Ben Idris*	SN.137	1972	442	M
Ben Lora	SN.43	1961	219	M
Ben Loyal	A.256	1958	296	M
Ben Lui	A.166	1971	469	M
Ben Meidie	A.319	1959	371	M
Ben Screel	A.105	1957	293	M
Ben Strome	SN.85	1962	282	M
Ben Tarbert	A.418	1960	280	M
Ben Vurie	SN.33	1961	282	M
Ben Wyvis	A.625	1974	370	M

* *Stern Trawler*

HUBERT JONES (TRAWLERS) LTD

Milford Haven & Swansea

FUNNEL: Yellow with black top.
HULL: Black.

Name	Port Registry	Date	Gross Tons	Engines
Georgina Wilson ex Fairy Cove-67	HL.10	1955	182	M
Sally McCabe ex Ocean Vim-55	YH.88	1930	127	M

W. H. KERR (SHIPS CHANDLERS) LTD
(Boston Group Holdings)

Milford Haven

FUNNEL: Red with black top.
HULL: Black with white line and red boot-topping.

Name	Port Registry	Date	Gross Tons	Engines
Boston Defiant ex Deeside-73	LT.517	1966	174	M
Boston Jaguar ex Dicketa-73	LT.463	1966	174	M
Deelux ex Ocean Lux-56	YH.84	1930	127	M
Willing Boys	LT.737	1930	147	M

THE KILVEY TRAWLING CO LTD

Swansea

FUNNEL:
HULL:

Name	Port Registry	Date	Gross Tons	Engines
Roger Bushell	BM.76	1946	117	M

I. LACE & A. LINCOLN

Lowestoft

FUNNEL: Red with or without black top.
HULL: Black with white line and red boot-topping.

Name	Port Registry	Date	Gross Tons	Engines
Ocean Scimitar ex Boston Scimitar -74	LT.100	1959	135	M

H. J. LAMPRELL & SONS LTD

Buntingford, Herts. & Milford Haven

FUNNEL: Various markings.
HULL: Blue or red.

Name	Port Registry	Date	Gross Tons	Engines
H. J. Lamprell:				
Fairway	LT.206	1958	175	M
Jadestar Gypsy ex Wroxham Queen-70	LT.53	1954	179	M
Platessa	LT.205	1946	112	M

LINDSEY TRAWLERS LTD

Grimsby

FUNNEL: Black with white band between red bands.
HULL: Black with red boot-topping.

Name	Port Registry	Date	Gross Tons	Engines
Lemberg	GY.664	1961	270	M
Lepanto	GY.662	1961	270	M
Lofoten	GY.684	1962	212	M
Loveden	GY.685	1962	212	M
Lucerne	GY.560	1959	324	M
Tom Grant	GY.1392	1962	262	M

MARINE BIOLOGICAL ASSOCIATION OF THE UNITED KINGDOM

Plymouth

FUNNEL: Red with black top.
HULL: Dark blue with red boot-topping.

Name	Port Registry	Date	Gross Tons	Engines
Research Trawler:				
Sarsia	PH.6	1953	319	M

J. MARR & SON LTD

Fleetwood

FUNNEL: Red with black top.
HULL: Yellow with dark red boot-topping.

Name	Port Registry	Date	Gross Tons	Engines
Benella	H.132	1958	789	M
Brucella	H.291	1953	678	M
Collena*	FD.221	1973	309	M
Cordella*	H.177	1973	1,238	M
Criscilla*	FD.261	1962	952	M(A)
Edwina	FD.162	1958	392	M
Farnella*	H.135	1972	1,469	M
Fyldea	FD.182	1973	582	M
Gavina	FD.126	1971	532	M
Irvana*	FD.141	1972	533	M

* Stern Trawler

J. Marr & Sons Ltd (Continued)

Name	Port Registry	Date	Gross Tons	Engines
Jacinta	FD.159	1972	599	M
Josena	FD.150	1957	392	M
Kirkella*	H.367	1965	1,714	DE
Lucida	H.403	1957	405	M
Luneda*	FD.134	1971	532	M
Marbella*	H.384	1966	1,786	DE
Maretta	FD.245	1965	439	M
Northella*	H.206	1973	1,238	M
Primella	H.98	1958	789	M
ex Northella-63				
Southella*	H.40	1969	1,144	M(A)
Starella	H.219	1960	606	M
Swanella*	H.421	1967	1,779	DE
Velia*	FD.220	1973	309	M
Westella	H.194	1960	779	M
Zonia	FD.236	1965	440	M

J. Marr (Aberdeen) Ltd:

Name	Port Registry	Date	Gross Tons	Engines
Coastal Emperor	A.456	1960	250	M
Dinas	FD.55	1956	439	M
Glen Affric	A.175	1971	114	M
Glen Carron	A.427	1973	299	M
Glen Coe	A.283	1973	299	M
Glen-Esk	A.184	1971	114	M
Glen Moriston	A.238	1973	299	M
Glen Uquhart	A.384	1973	301	M
Paramount	A.309	1959	250	M
Partisan	A.310	1959	250	M

Forward Motor Trawlers Ltd, Aberdeen:

Name	Port Registry	Date	Gross Tons	Engines
Corena	FD.173	1959	353	M
Jacamar	A.525	1961	237	M

Radiation Fishing Co Ltd, Aberdeen:

Name	Port Registry	Date	Gross Tons	Engines
Radiation	A.115	1957	139	M

* *Stern Trawler*

F. McALINDEN & RICHARD DONNAN

Whitehaven

FUNNEL: Yellow with brown letters "McA" in brown oval ring.
HULL: Black with red boot-topping.

Name	Port Registry	Date	Gross Tons	Engines
Quo Vadis DM.	A.778	1972	359	M

MINISTRY OF AGRICULTURE, FISHERIES AND FOOD, FISHERIES DEPARTMENT

London

FUNNEL: Yellow with black top.
HULL: Black with white line and red boot-topping.

Name	Port Registry	Date	Gross Tons	Engines
Fishery Research Vessels:				
Based Grimsby for Distant Water Research:				
Cirolana*	GY.156	1970	1,731	DE(A)
Based Lowestoft for Middle and Near Water Research:				
Clione	LT.421	1961	495	M
Corella*	LT.767	1967	459	M(A)
Based Aberdeen for Handling and Preservation of fish at sea Research:				
Sir William Hardy	A.45	1955	418	DE

* Stern Trawler

MITCHELL BROS. LTD

Lowestoft

FUNNEL: As below.
HULL: Grey with white whalemouth and red boot-topping.

Name	Port Registry	Date	Gross Tons	Engines
Jackora Ltd (Funnel: Blue with white letter "M"):				
Jacklyn	LT.434	1962	162	M
Ocean Breeze	LT.341	1927	118	M
Merbreeze Ltd (Funnel: Yellow with houseflag):				
Merbreeze	LT.365	1931	122	M
Mitchell's Tritonia Ltd (Funnel: Blue with houseflag):				
Tritonia	LT.188	1930	123	M
Scattan Ltd (Funnel: Yellow with houseflag):				
Hosanna	LT.167	1930	140	M

Top : LUCIDA, J. Marr & Son Ltd *J. Clarkson*

JACKLYN, Jackora Ltd *B. G. Banham*

JOHN B. MORGAN & OTHERS

Peterhead

FUNNEL:
HULL:

Name	Port Registry	Date	Gross Tons	Engines
Seringa	PD.95	1972	107	M
William Morgan & Others:				
Sundari	PD.93	1972	107	M

J. MUIR

Anstruther

FUNNEL:
HULL:

Name	Port Registry	Date	Gross Tons	Engines
Ocean Dawn	KY.371	1956	131	M
David W. Muir & Others:				
Ocean Sceptre	KY.378	1969	111	M

NEWINGTON TRAWLERS LTD

Hull

FUNNEL: Grey with black top separated by broad blue band.
HULL: Black with white line and red boot-topping.

Name	Port Registry	Date	Gross Tons	Engines
C. S. Forester*	H.86	1969	768	M
Hammond Innes*	H.180	1972	897	M
Joseph Conrad	H.161	1958	740	SR
Peter Scott	H.103	1949	666	SR
ex Primella-57				
Somerset Maugham	H.329	1961	789	M

* *Stern Trawler*

Newington Trawlers Ltd (Continued)

Name	Port Registry	Date	Gross Tons	Engines
Mike Burton Ltd:				
Rudyard Kipling ex Tarchon-73, Swanella-62	H.152	1952	823	SR

* *Stern Trawlers*

NEWTON TRAWLERS LTD

Grimsby

FUNNEL : Red with narrow black top.
HULL : Black with white line and red boot-topping.

Name	Port Registry	Date	Gross Tons	Engines
Volesus ex Abunda	GY.188	1956	577	M

NORRARD TRAWLERS LTD

Milford Haven

FUNNEL : Yellow with blue star.
HULL : Grey with red boot-topping, or black with white line and red boot-topping.

Name	Port Registry	Date	Gross Tons	Engines
Bryher	LT.371	1961	166	M
Constant Star	M.133	1962	140	M
Norrard Star	M.44	1956	167	M
Piction Sea Eagle	M.68	1958	197	M
Piction Sealion	M.22	1956	166	M

NORTH STAR FISHING CO LTD

Aberdeen

FUNNEL: Grey with black top separated by red over white bands.
HULL: Black with red boot-topping.

Name	Port Registry	Date	Gross Tons	Engines
Parkroyd	A.161	1960	310	M

J. R. PERKES & OTHERS

Brixham

FUNNEL: Orange with blue cowl.
HULL: Orange.

Name	Port Registry	Date	Gross Tons	Engines
Jannie-Marie	BM.III	1959	107	M

DONALD C. POLLACK & OTHERS

Aberdeen

FUNNEL: Black.
HULL: Green with red boot-topping.

Name	Port Registry	Date	Gross Tons	Engines
Seaward Venture	A.509	1960	215	M

PUTFORD ENTERPRISES LTD
(Boston Group Holdings)

Lowestoft & Paignton

FUNNEL: Black with orange band.
HULL: Black.

Name	Port Registry	Date	Gross Tons	Engines
Ada Kirby	LT.72	1958	126	M
Arduous	LT.400	1944	116	M
Boston Seafoam	FD.42	1956	398	M
Dreadnought	A.377	1960	163	M
Eastleigh	LT.76	1956	239	M
ex Boston Harrier-72				
Arcadia Snowbird-				
68, launched as				
Boston Britannia				
Idena	A.793	1953	317	M
Jean Marthe	FD.233	1948	187	M
Margaret Christina	LT.331	1960	137	M
Mincarlo	LT.412	1962	166	M
Woodleigh	LT.240	1960	199	M

JOHN R. REID & OTHERS

Gardenstown

FUNNEL:
HULL:

Name	Port Registry	Date	Gross Tons	Engines
Dauntless Star	LT.367	1948	133	M
ex Swiftburn-58,				
Boston Swift-57,				
Sunlit Waters-52				

SIR THOMAS ROBINSON & SON (GRIMSBY) LTD

Grimsby

FUNNEL: Black with red, white and blue tricolour houseflag.
HULL: Black with white line and red boot-topping.

Name	Port Registry	Date	Gross Tons	Engines
Ephesian	GY.604	1959	328	M
Galilaean	GY.603	1959	328	M
Judaean	GY.644	1960	272	M
Olivean	GY.92	1954	252	M
Philadelphian	GY.636	1960	272	M
Thessalonian	GY.112	1955	254	M
Tiberian	GY.673	1961	283	M
Dominion Steam Fishing Co Ltd (Black letter "D" on white of houseflag):				
Priscillian	GY.672	1961	283	M
Onward Steam Fishing Co Ltd (Black letter "O" on white of houseflag):				
Rhodesian	GY.457	1957	331	M
Samarian	GY.445	1957	331	M

DAVID W. ROSS & OTHERS

Aberdeen

FUNNEL:
HULL:

Name	Port Registry	Date	Gross Tons	Engines
Kingsdale	A.437	1973	117	M

E. SALTHOUSE & J. R. BRACKENBURY

Fleetwood

FUNNEL: Red with narrow black top.
HULL: Green with red boot-topping.

Name	Port Registry	Date	Gross Tons	Engines
Moreleigh	HL.160	1946	112	M

SEAFRIDGE LTD

Hull & London

FUNNEL: Grey with black top separated by broad blue band.
HULL: Black with white line and red boot-topping.

Name	Port Registry	Date	Gross Tons	Engines
Seafridge Osprey*	H.137	1972	878	M
Seafridge Petrel*	H.175	1973	878	M
Seafridge Skua*	H.138	1972	878	M

* *Stern Freezer Trawler*
Fleet managed by Newington Trawlers Ltd

PETER SLEIGHT TRAWLERS LTD

Grimsby

FUNNEL: Black with blue letter "P" on white band between narrow blue bands.
HULL: Black with white line and red boot-topping.

Name	Port Registry	Date	Gross Dons	Engines
Fiskerton ex Balmoral-64	GY.676	1962	199	M
Scampton	GY.166	1961	214	M
Waddington	GY.680	1962	230	M

MALCOLM SMITH LTD

Aberdeen

FUNNEL: Brown with black top.
HULL: Green with red boot-topping.

Name	Port Registry	Date	Gross Tons	Engines
Loch Brora	A.198	1958	191	M

JAMES STEVENSON

London

FUNNEL: Red.
HULL: Black with red boot-topping.

Name	Port Registry	Date	Gross Tons	Engines
Peaceful Star	A.61	1931	121	M

STEVENSON & SONS

Newlyn

FUNNEL: Black with blue band.
HULL: Grey with red boot-topping.

Name	Port Registry	Date	Gross Tons	Engines
Anthony Stevenson:				
Elizabeth Caroline	PZ.293	1946	112	M
William Stevenson:				
Marie Claire	PZ.295	1946	112	M
Jacqueline S. Webster:				
Elizabeth Ann Webster	PZ.291	1946	109	M

WILLIAM M. G. TAIT & OTHERS

Fraserburgh

FUNNEL:
HULL:

Name	Port Registry	Date	Gross Tons	Engines
David John	A.169	1969	110	M
A. Tait & Sons				
Comrades	A.	1974	165	M
Xmas Rose	A.	1973	110	M(A)

TALISMAN TRAWLERS LTD
Lowestoft & West Hartlepool

FUNNEL: Yellow with black letter "G".
HULL: Black with red boot-topping.

Name	Port Registry	Date	Gross Tons	Engines
Barton Queen	LT.298	1957	178	M
Boltby Queen	LT.161	1973		M
Carlton Queen	LT.363	1961	196	M
Norton Queen	LT.356	1958	197	M
Waveney Queen	LT.16	1968	239	M
Wilton Queen	LT.145	1960	199	M
Talisman Trawlers (North Sea) Ltd:				
Bentley Queen	LT.32	1971	120	M
Farnham Queen ex Blacktail-65	LT.502	1961	246	M
Filby Queen	LT.155	1955	181	M
Ormesby Queen	LT.88	1954	181	M
Oulton Queen ex Dorade-65	LT.503	1961	246	M
Ripley Queen	LT.30	1970	284	M
Underley Queen	LT.31	1971	284	M
Yoxford Queen ex Sailfin-65	LT.501	1962	390	M

VIGILANCE FISHING CO LTD
Aberdeen

FUNNEL: Red with two narrow yellow bands.
HULL: Black with red boot-topping.

Name	Port Registry	Date	Gross Tons	Engines
Glenstruan	A.200	1958	183	M

JOHN N. WARD & SONS LTD
Fleetwood

FUNNEL:
HULL: Blue with red boot-topping.

Name	Port Registry	Date	Gross Tons	Engines
Resound* ex Merrydale-73	FD.104	1970	145	M(A)

* Stern Trawler

John N. Ward & Sons Ltd (Continued)

Name	Port Registry	Date	Gross Tons	Engines
John N. Ward & Sons and Banks Ltd:				
Rosamunda ex Rosa Maris-73	FD.284	1970	109	M

* *Stern Trawler*

WELSH SEA FOODS LTD

Bangor

FUNNEL: Orange with black top and black "WSF".
HULL: Black with red boot-topping.

Name	Port Registry	Date	Gross Tons	Engines
Segontium	LO.115	1943	192	M

JAMES WILSON

Fleetwood & Buckie

FUNNEL: Black with narrow blue band and separate blue, red & white monogram device.
HULL: Black with white line and red boot-topping.

Name	Port Registry	Date	Gross Tons	Engines
Andrew Wilson* ex Virtue Pettit-68	M.73	1959	197	M
Brenda Wilson ex Granby Queen-67	LT.80	1954	181	M
David Wilson ex Star of Devon	A.513	1961	224	M
William & James *Wilson:*				
Hazelglen	BCK.145	1918	107	M

* *Oil rig safety duty*

JAMES M. WILSON & OTHERS

Anstruther

FUNNEL:
HULL:

Name	Port Registry	Date	Gross Tons	Engines
Anna Christina ex Suffolk Maid-71	KY.338	1957	130	M

GEORGE WOOD (ABERDEEN) LTD

Aberdeen

FUNNEL: Cream with black top separated by narrow red band.
HULL: Black with red boot-topping.

Name	Port Registry	Date	Gross Tons	Engines
Bracondene	A.590	1961	215	M
Emma Wood ex Granton Kestrel-63, Teresa Watterston- 58	A.735	1956	197	M
Heather K. Wood ex Elizabeth Paton- 72	A.723	1960	220	M
Ailsa Craig Fishing Co Ltd:				
Clovella	A.63	1957	238	M
Craiglynne	A.324	1960	163	M
George R. Wood ex Netherley-70	A.465	1960	220	M
Stratherrick	A.763	1960	237	M
Wilronwood Fishing Co Ltd:				
Boston Sea Hawk	A.178	1953	180	M
Wilronwood	A.546	1961	166	M
Wm. Wood:				
Braconhill	A.138	1956	274	M

THE JOHN WOOD GROUP (ABERDEEN) LTD
(Associated with Boston Deep Sea Fishing Co Ltd)

Aberdeen

FUNNEL: Red with black top and houseflag.
HULL: Black with red boot-topping.

Name	Port Registry	Date	Gross Tons	Engines
Aberdeen Motor Trawlers Ltd:				
Admiral Nelson ex Princess Royal-63	A.469	1960	300	M
Admiral Vian ex Mannofield-62	A.580	1961	226	M
Aberdeen Near Water Trawler Ltd:				
Aberdeen Venturer	A.488	1960	298	M
Boston Victor ex Woodside-63	LT.473	1959	190	M
Japonica	A.524	1961	234	M
Leswood	A.443	1960	237	M
The Ashley Fishing Co Ltd:				
Dalewood	A.481	1960	234	M
Jasmin	A.523	1961	234	M
Burwood Fishing Co Ltd:				
Burwood	A.547	1961	249	M
Clarkwood	A.557	1961	249	M
The Don Fishing Co Ltd & Others:				
Isadale	A.678	1971	117	M
Jasire	A.373	1972	115	M
Maureen June	A.372	1972	115	M
Margona	A.381	1973	119	M
Sealgair	A.313	1971	117	M
Strathella ex Fairfield-73	A.361	1962	207	M
Leslie Fishing Co Ltd:				
Janwood	A.457	1960	250	M
Lorwood	A.400	1960	237	M
Milwood	A.472	1960	250	M
Starwood	A.431	1960	237	M

Top: BRACONDENE, George Wood (Aberdeen) Ltd *J. K. Byass*
Centre: ALEXANDER BRUCE, Minerva Fishing Co Ltd *T. J. M. Wood*
Bottom: WYRE DEFENCE, Wyre Trawlers Ltd *J. Clarkson*

WOOD & BRUCE LTD
(British United Trawlers (Aberdeen) Ltd)

Aberdeen

FUNNEL: Red with deep black top with varying additions of subsidiary companies.
HULL: Black with white line and red boot-topping.

Name	Port Registry	Date	Gross Tons	Engines
Glencairn	A.491	1960	228	M
Glenisla	A.282	1959	279	M
Clova Fishing Co Ltd:				
Clova	A.417	1960	281	M
Crusader Fishing Co Ltd:				
Red Crusader	A.240	1958	274	M
Minerva Fishing Co Ltd:				
Alexander Bruce	A.141	1957	274	M
David Wood	A.142	1957	274	M
Strathcoe Fishing Co Ltd:				
Strathdon	A.234	1958	275	M

WYRE TRAWLERS LTD
(British United Trawlers Ltd)

Fleetwood

FUNNEL: Black with two narrow white bands.
HULL: Black with white line and red boot-topping.

Name	Port Registry	Date	Gross Tons	Engines
Wyre Captain ex Loch Melfort-68, Prince Charles-57	FD.228	1953	490	M
Wyre Conqueror	FD.187	1959	398	M

Wyre Trawlers Ltd (Continued)

Name	Port Registry	Date	Gross Tons	Engines
Wyre Defence	FD.37	1956	338	M
Wyre Majestic	FD.433	1956	338	M
Wyre Revenge	FD.432	1956	338	M
Wyre Vanguard	FD.36	1955	338	M
Wyre Victory	FD.181	1960	398	M
Macdavitte Ltd, Hull:				
Wyre Corsair	FD.27	1953	442	M
Wyre Gleaner	FD.269	1953	442	M

ADDENDA

Company Changes

New Companies:

Name	Built	Tons	Length	Breadth	Speed	Engines
Ben Line Ltd, Edinburgh, Chemical Tankers						
Benvenue	1974	2,400dw			13	M(A)
New (3)	1975/76	2,400dw			13	M(A)
Concord Leasing Ltd, London						
Helena Jayne	1956	382	160	26	9	M(A)
ex Viking-74						
Johanca	1957	500			10	M(A)
Tinda	1957	453			9	M(A)
Ensign Freight Services Ltd, London						
Pattree	1961	424	168	29	9	M(A)
ex Barbara-74						
Guernsey Coasters Ltd, Guernsey C.I.						
Bandick	1961	250	139	25	8	M(A)
ex Christine-74						
R.A. Glass & Others, Rochester						
Alberson	1956	324	146	28	8	M(A)
ex Rysum-73,						
Forelle-71,						
Helge-64						
G. W. Holdings (Frendo London Ltd) London						
Frendo Faith	1974	1,599	219	44	12	M(A)
Frendo Grace	1974	1,599	219	44	12	M(A)
Frendo Hope	1974	1,599	219	44	12	M(A)
Frendo Pride	1974	1,599	219	44	12	M(A)
Frendo Spirit	1974	1,599	219	44	12	M(A)
Frendo Star	1974	1,599	219	44	12	M(A)
R. & H. Hall Ltd, Dublin						
New (2)	1975/76	1,275			12	M(A)
Iffie Corineus Lines Ltd, Helston						
Ekpan Chieftain	1962	467	168	28	10	M(A)
ex Nora-74						
A. J. Kinnear, Swansea						
Markab Star	1956	500			9	M(A)
ex Markab-74						
N. E. Murray, London						
Trent	1931	135	100	20	8	M(A)
Whitbury Shipping Ltd, Rochester						
Borelly	1956	430	167	27	10	M(A)

VESSEL SALES, TRANSFERS AND RENAMINGS

Sea Containers Ltd, London. The following vessels have been renamed consequent upon charterers preference:

Tiber,	1,599/70	renamed	City of Naples
Tua,	1,599/70	renamed	City of Florence
Tormes,	1,599/70	renamed	City of Oporto
Tamega,	1,598/71	renamed	City of Genoa
Tagus,	1,598/70	renamed	City of Lisbon
Tronto,	1,587/71	renamed	City of La Spezia
Mondego,	1,598/72	renamed	City of Venice
Minho,	1,578/69	renamed	City of Milan
Britis,	1,590/71	renamed	Captain Paddon

Ellerman Lines Ltd, London. The following vessels have been renamed to fit in with new company policy:

Rapallo,	3,402/60	renamed	City of Limassol
Sorrento,	1,523/67	renamed	City of Sparta
Silvio,	1,523/68	renamed	City of Patras
Sangro,	1,523/68	renamed	City of Ankara
Salerno,	1,599/65	renamed	City of Corinth

Western Shipping Ltd, Plymouth

Treviscoe, 494/52, has been sold to Alba Shipping Co (Le Blond Shipping Co) South Shields. Renamed Beauly Firth.

W. G. S. Crouch Ltd, Greenhithe

William Spearing, 136/45, has been sold to C. Crawley Ltd, Gravesend. Renamed Aquaseal.

George Wood (Aberdeen) Ltd, Aberdeen

Emma Wood, 197/56, has been sold to Putford Enterprises Ltd, Lowestoft. Renamed Northleigh.

Putford Enterprises Ltd, Lowestoft

Boston Seafoam, 398/56, has been renamed Westleigh and subsequently Arkinholm. Idena, 317/53, has been renamed Falkirk.

Boston Deep Sea Fisheries Ltd, Hull (Brixham Trawlers Ltd)

Boston Nimrod, 315/56, has been renamed Glenfinnan

Iago Steam Trawler Co Ltd, Fleetwood

Boston Invader, 407/55, has been renamed Inverlochy

Safetyships Ltd, Aberdeen

Ocean Trust, 113/57, has been renamed Tippermuir

INDEX